Praise for *Happen to Your Career*

**HAPPEN
TO YOUR
CAREER**

Meet Scott

SCOTT ANTHONY BARLOW is CEO of Happen to Your Career and host of the *Happen to Your Career Podcast*, which has been listened to over 3 million times across 159 countries and is the largest career change podcast in the world. As a former HR leader, Scott has interviewed over two thousand people for jobs and completely rejects the way most organizations choose to do work. He's a nerd for self development, human behavior, and monthlong travel to other countries. Scott lives in Washington State with his wife and three kids. Scott also dislikes writing in the third person, but he really hopes you'll like this book.

An Unconventional Approach to Career Change and Meaningful Work

HAPPEN TO *your* CAREER

SCOTT ANTHONY BARLOW

HAPPEN PUBLISHING

Some names and identifying details have been
changed to protect the privacy of individuals.

Happen to Your Career® is a registered trademark
of Happen to Your Career LLC.

Cataloguing in publication information is
available from Library and Archives Canada.
ISBN 979-8-9854912-0-3 (paperback)
ISBN 979-8-9854912-1-0 (ebook)
ISBN 979-8-9854912-2-7 (audiobook)

Happen Publishing

Produced by Page Two
pagetwo.com

Edited by Sarah Brohman
Copyedited by Jenny Govier
Cover design by Peter Cocking
Interior design by Fiona Lee

happentoyourcareer.com

To Alyssa, Mackenzie, Camden, and Grayson.
You're my driving reason for
why I "happen to" anything at all.

Contents

Introduction: My Why

Y WIFE, Alyssa, and I moved to Portland, Oregon, in 2005 after I'd accepted a highly paid but unexciting job as a regional manager. We bought a house that was twice as expensive as anything my parents had ever owned. In my new job I was managing a team of twenty people. If I did well in my first year, the company promised me a BMW. I felt safe, successful, optimistic.

But it didn't last.

My commute to work was three hours a day. My work schedule was seventy to eighty hours per week. I didn't have weekends. I didn't have time off. I never saw Alyssa. I couldn't focus, I couldn't work, and I was scared. I gained nearly fifty pounds by self-medicating with food. I developed panic attacks. (I didn't even know what panic attacks were before this!)

It was bad. So bad that I began looking for a way out. Many days in a row I seriously considered the window. Not kidding. It was only two stories. If I "fell" (jumped) out the window, I'd probably just break my legs. They'd have to give me some time off . . . right? Would insurance cover that? Was that fraud? What if I got in trouble? Or got fired? I felt a panic attack coming on. I decided against the window.

Next to the office was a burger place. One day I decided to stress-eat myself sick and then tell them I needed to go home. I sat down and had three burgers, fries, and a huckleberry milkshake big enough to fill a bathtub. It didn't work. I got sick, but just nauseated enough to sit at my desk, writhing in pain, pretending to answer emails. Not enough to go home. Damn.

I was trapped. Wife. House. Car of my dreams. No way out. But I had to keep going.

I went on this way for a year. Then one day, on the way to work, I had a panic attack so intense that I knew I was dying. In the car. Alone. On Interstate 5, in bumper-to-bumper traffic, with no way for an ambulance to reach me. I could see the headlines: "Fat loser dies in car because the real world was too hard for him. He is survived by his wife and his student loans."

I didn't die. But I decided something had to change.

I brought my concerns to my boss, who listened politely. Three weeks later, he assembled my team, called me into his office, and told me I was fired. But he did give me a choice: I could walk into the other room and tell the twelve people working for me that I was leaving, and he would give me three months' severance. Or I could walk out the door without telling them and get two weeks' pay. I needed the money. One last humiliation. I stood in front of my team and told them I was leaving. There were tears (mine). I was a failure. I apologized. I left. Me and my three months' severance.

This was horrible, and I wouldn't wish it on anyone, but I'm not sharing this story with you because I want you to feel sorry for me. Actually, it became one of the best gifts I could ever have received. Driving home in the rain, I made myself a promise. I decided I would never live like that again. I knew I had to figure out how to do work that didn't stress me out to the max. There had to be something out there that didn't make me feel this way. Maybe even something that I actually enjoyed? This was my why.

This single decision sent me on a decade-long journey of learning how to live without settling in my career and all aspects of life. I wanted to learn how to live what was most important to me; I didn't want to be thrown around by life and my work circumstances. I wanted to understand how and why a few people are able to grab the reins and live the way they want to, while others feel like they are forever at the mercy of whatever is thrown their way.

This book is for you if you don't want to settle and have often wondered if there could be more out there for you. This book is certainly for you if you want to identify and do your career in a much more meaningful way, a way that feeds you and fulfills you. But, just as importantly, a way where you get to use your talents, strengths, and skills to help others so that you're getting just as much back.

To be clear, this book is not for you if you just want a "better job." It's also not for you if you only want to be paid more. A better job and pay are easy in comparison to the process this book lays out. You must be excited about the prospect of doing work that is meaningful to you and contributes to others in this world in far greater ways than what you might be doing right now, while getting well compensated.

The part I didn't tell you about my story is that I had a great job. Great pay, great people I worked with, great training and opportunities. There were many wonderful things about it. My good friend who also worked at the company loved it. He stayed around an additional fifteen years and eventually became the president.

Even though it was a great fit for him, the company was most definitely not a great fit for me. And that's what this book is really about: how to relentlessly find your own fit. Your own version of what extraordinary is for you. I promise it's drastically different for you compared to me or the next person. That's okay. The socially accepted norms that dictate what makes a great career don't often align with what humans really need. So, whether you're already in a good job and have had a good career but want to find what's next for you, or whether you're in a dismal situation that you want to escape, this book will help you uncover your ideal version of your career and help you understand what it takes to get there. It will teach you what I've learned searching for career fulfillment since 2006.

Over the years, I've sat for over one hundred job interviews and changed careers many times, even moving from operations to human resources leadership. I've conducted over two thousand job interviews and learned executive and leadership coaching. Along the way, I held many "dream jobs," but then my dreams would change or evolve, and I would move on. And throughout the process, I was learning, growing, building my skills, and homing in on what I really wanted.

In 2012, I started my company Happen to Your Career (HTYC) to help people like you find career fulfillment. Since then, we've helped thousands of people find their ideal careers and transition to extraordinary work. In 2013 I began the *Happen to Your Career Podcast*, which has been called one of the best career podcasts by media outlets like *Forbes* and Lifehacker and has had millions of downloads. My work has been featured globally on MSNBC, Glassdoor, and The Muse and in hundreds of other publications and podcasts. I regularly get paid to speak at universities and organizations about meaningful work, strengths, and happiness.

In this book I will share what we've uncovered at HTYC that works for our clients. I will also share what doesn't work. You will get both the practical applications and the scientific research supporting them. As near as I can tell, there is no other company or person in the world that has access to so much direct information on how real people make seemingly impossible career changes to meaningful, well-paid work. I wrote this book so that I could pass this knowledge to you.

Work can be unhealthy for many of us. But it doesn't have to be. I've seen what it can do on the positive side. It can feed you—literally, because, you know, it pays money that can magically turn into food—but figuratively as well. When done well, work can help you thrive.

I wrote this book to help you get to work that allows you to flourish, to create an extraordinary career and life for yourself. And not because you have to, but because you choose when, where, and how you work, and no longer spend years of your life tolerating a poor fit—or worse, a good fit that keeps you comfortably unhappy.

But I have a bigger purpose in writing this book. It's the same purpose that my organization serves: my team and I want to change how work is done. We want to make work freakin' great for humans. We work with individuals to do this, but my secret mission in writing this book is to teach you what we as humans need to make work fulfilling so that you can go find (or create) your own place in the world that is great for you. Then, once you're there, we want you to help transform the organizations you're a part of to make them better for humans, too. I wrote this book for you, but it's bigger than just you. We all need you to make this change for yourself.

In this book, you're going to read about the countless ways professionals have found their way to thriving in their careers. You'll read about how one woman created her own role drinking wine, writing about it, and running communications for companies she loved. And about how a lawyer who spent a decade trying to remove himself from law successfully transitioned to content strategy. How an engineer made a career change upwards instead of laterally while moving cities, jobs, and industries. We'll reveal how an executive discovered that work could be fun for the first time in his twenty-plus-year career. You'll also learn how people from every profession build plans for career change using the same principles that allow airplanes to arrive safely every time. You'll learn that it is possible to have a career you're enamored with that is good for you, your family, your bank account, and even your long-term health.

All this is very possible, but let's first take a look at what's at stake if you don't act.

PART ONE

IS CAREER CHANGE FOR YOU?

1

Why You Must Change

*If you dare nothing, then when the day
is over, nothing is all you will have gained.*

NEIL GAIMAN

I N 2020 I was in San Diego with my wife, Alyssa, celebrating twenty-one years together. We had a few hours before heading to the airport and flying home to our three kids, so we met up with Michael, a former client, at a diner overlooking Pacific Beach. He had spent the morning photographing the ocean.

This meet-up took place only a few months after Michael had accepted a new role as an independent mortgage broker, a completely different career from the one where he had struggled, and one Michael had never imagined he would land in. But he was deliriously happy, smiling and telling me and Alyssa how much better his life was than it had been in years. "I still have trouble accepting that work can be enjoyable or even fun," he said. But he was learning. He genuinely enjoyed the work and his coworkers. He loved the organization. He was using his strengths, learning new skills, and making good money. The new role truly fit him, and he was thriving. This is the happy end of his career change, but a few years previously, Michael wasn't thriving—he was dying.

Michael had ascended the corporate ladder at a major movie studio unimpeded for eighteen years. He started in 2001 as a senior financial analyst, and by 2012 he was a vice president. His last role was VP of worldwide distribution finance. Sounds like an important job, right? It was. Michael managed the financial projections for billions of dollars, as well as a large global team.

But something was drastically wrong. In the past year, Michael had lost twenty pounds. He couldn't sleep. He couldn't exercise. He left work regularly past 11 pm and spent many weekends at home alone, trying to catch up with work or paralyzed with anxiety. Medically, there was nothing wrong with him. He didn't have cancer, or a tapeworm, or a mental illness. What he had was a job in finance at a large entertainment company in Los Angeles—and it was killing him.

Michael had always loved working at the studio. He loved movies, was well paid, and was challenged by his projects and responsibilities. He frequently met with the most senior executives at the studio and traveled to Europe many times for projects. It was exciting and prestigious, especially in LA. Try telling someone in LA that you're a doctor or a lawyer. *Oh, that's nice.* Now tell them you work for a major film studio. *Ooh—I wanna take you to BRUNCH.*

Michael had gotten himself a job in the entertainment industry, almost on a whim, and had never left. But honestly, he didn't care that much about the studio aura. He just loved accounting and finance. He enjoyed the feeling of harmony he got from putting things in order, keeping things in balance, like a Zen rock garden, but with numbers instead of rocks. His promotions had given him huge amounts of responsibility, and although this wasn't new for him, lately something was drastically different.

His recent promotion no longer felt like a Zen rock garden. Now it was distressingly the opposite. It was more like huge, smoldering meteors falling out of the sky, threatening to crush you, your dog, your car, and everyone you care about.

Every new film, television show, limited series, or digital short is an entirely new product with its own unit economics. The movie production process may go wildly over budget, or the movie may come out but no one wants to see it. And when that happens, look out. The accounting department and people like Michael can basically give up on the idea of leaving the office for the next month. The entire year's plans, projections, and estimates are out the window and must be completely revised.

After years of this, Michael was exhausted. In other words, what was once a great career for him had been turned upside down and replaced with the most misaligned situation imaginable. But that's not when he left the company. He waited around for another three years.

You might ask yourself, Why did he stay? Couldn't he see what was at stake? Why didn't he want to change?

So many reasons: Michael still felt a sense of responsibility to his team. He wanted to see them advance. He also felt a sense of responsibility to the studio. He didn't think anyone else could do his job, or certainly not as well as he did it. Finally, he was sure that things would get better. They had to because after so many years, Michael couldn't conceive of another job. Everything outside the studio seemed like darkness. *Pull yourself together*, he told himself. He was lucky to have a high-paying job at a major film studio. Thousands of people would love to have his job. Who was he to complain? Work is *supposed* to be hard, right? That's why they call it "work."

Many of us accept a certain definition of what work is in our society. We believe that work conflicts with everything else we might want in life. So much so that almost nobody in the world has work they love that pays well and is meaningful. Somehow, we're okay with this. We even accept this as normal, and then beat ourselves up for wanting something different. Unfortunately, few people ask why it still has to be this way, given the recent changes in the work world. Instead of asking, "What do I want and need from work?" the question we're asking is, "What is the best situation I believe I can get?"

That's why this book is about answering the singular question that has fascinated me since 2005: How do certain people create careers they love, but not at the expense of the rest of their life? I wanted to learn about *those* people, who love their work *and* enjoy their life *and* get well compensated on top of it. Not the people who excel in their career but are absentee parents. And not the people who sacrifice all their relationships to be better at their craft. But the people who define success on their own terms; the people who know what they want and find a way against all impossibilities to make it happen by prioritizing the needs of work and life in a healthy way. And I wanted to understand what this specific group of people was doing differently than the entire rest of the world.

I call these people Happy High Achievers. I first began studying this group of high-performing people in 2006 for my own interest. I continued to study them later when I started my company, Happen to Your Career. This book will show you how high performers—hardworking, intelligent, successful, real people—change their careers to become Happy High Achievers. It will show you the misconceptions that can keep you stuck in roles and organizations that don't fit. It will help you identify your key strengths and find a role that allows you to use your strengths so you can feel more fulfilled in your work.

To do that, I'm going to explore the science behind the entire process of career change and offer you tactics you can use on your own journey. I'll also share some success stories that will illustrate how people really do happen to their career. But it is important to note that this book isn't a step-by-step guide.

One of the biggest challenges we've observed at HTYC is that the process of career change does not consist of the same set of steps for everyone. Over the years we've noticed that people who get to do work that matters to them, work that fits their strengths and allows them to experience growth in ways that feel fulfilling, are doing things differently, even unconventionally. What this means is if you ever see a step-by-step guide that promises a solution to every one of your meaningful work problems, rest assured that it's incomplete at best and a farce at worst.

Normal Work Is No Longer Working

In a world where only 4 percent of people have what Gallup would call "great jobs," and even fewer people think their work is meaningful and fulfilling, I believe work can be so much more for so many people.[1] It must be so much more, because what you do for a living is inextricably linked to your relationships, your finances, your time, your demeanor, and the energy with which you interact with your family.

This book is all about how high achievers find meaningful, well-paid work without starting over. Specifically, what do these individuals do to make career changes? And what are they doing differently than the rest of us who are tolerating "normal" (read good-enough or even not-so-great) work or whose struggles seem to go unnoticed?

Case in point: Michael was clearly unwell, but no one seemed to notice. Maybe his colleagues were too busy trying to manage their own stress. Or maybe they just didn't care. As Michael withered away out of sheer misery, no one asked him that simple question: *Are you okay?* Instead, they continued to pile on new responsibilities.

Now, step back and think about the absurdity of this situation. What was Michael thinking, staying in a job that was killing him? Sure, he liked accounting, and he liked the entertainment business, but he'd never joined the company expecting to stay there for his entire career, much less to die there as a martyr for studio accounting. And what do you think about a place where an eighteen-year employee, a senior executive, exhibits symptoms of a serious illness and no one notices or cares? How do you watch a forty-something man of average height and weight lose twenty pounds and not think that something is wrong? Certainly, any reasonable person would look at this man day after day and think he needed medical attention. Instead, they looked at this dying man and said, "He's ready for a more challenging role." Michael's story should be shocking, but it's not—it's typical.

But before you write off this particular movie studio as a terrible place to work at, as it turns out, this is a company that is well liked by its employees. At the time of this writing 80 percent of reviewers on Glassdoor would recommend this company to a friend, and 89 percent approve of the company's CEO. So what's really going on here?

Michael's behavior and the movie studio's behavior fit with how we are trained to think about work: Work sucks. Work is painful. Work is physically punishing. Work is depressing. Work is hell. Work is supposed to make you feel like shit. You're supposed to sacrifice your goals, hobbies, interests, needs (in Michael's case, *eating food*) for the good of the team and the company. And somewhere on the other side of all of this mindless suffering is an abstract achievement called "success"— whatever that means.

Is this "normal"?

As a career coach and CEO since 2013, and as a leader in HR at many organizations for the decade before that, I've listened to and witnessed many stories like Michael's—told by smart, talented, driven, hardworking people who were crippled by jobs they knew no longer fit them. We're talking about afflictions like temporary blindness, seizures, acid reflux, chronic back pain, anxiety disorders, eating disorders, clinical depression, and suicidal thoughts. These are not Happy High Achievers. Instead, they push themselves to the breaking point rather than admit they need to change careers. What's more amazing is that for many of these people, including Michael, when they changed their careers, their illnesses went away.

Reaching the Fed-Up Point

Does it seem to you that there must be something better out there, but you have no idea what it is or how to find it?

It's not easy for driven, hardworking, successful people to convince themselves to change careers. They're often committed to the organization they work for, to their team, or to using their graduate degrees. They have to reach the "fed-up point," and that can take years. Arriving at the fed-up point is often the result of a double-trigger process. The first trigger is realizing that they're unhappy and want to change their career. That seems like it should be enough to convince them to change, but it's not. They need a second trigger, usually an external event that propels them into action.

The pivotal event that convinced Michael to leave the studio took place after he'd accepted his last promotion and had been in the role for months. He walked into a meeting with two senior VPs, and one of them looked at Michael and asked, "Hey, are you going to jump off the building?" Although they may have been joking, this was a wakeup call for Michael. Not because he'd spent the past couple of months feeling sick during most of his waking hours. Nope, it was because before that meeting, he'd had real thoughts about jumping off a building.

Michael had accepted the additional responsibilities because he didn't want to miss the opportunity for new challenges and growth. He'd stayed at the company because he felt responsibility to his team and because even though the work had nearly doubled, he still believed he needed to figure it out. The VP's question made him realize that the situation was far more serious.

After that meeting, he went to see his doctor, who confirmed he was so anxious and exhausted that he might not physically survive this level of stress for much longer. Michael gave his two weeks' notice with no idea of what he wanted to do next except regain his health. That decision probably saved his life and certainly made it much better than the one he was living.

I live for stories like Michael's. They inspire me to help people who are unhappy or settling in their careers find work that truly fits them so they can thrive. But Michael's story is not a fairy tale. The world of work has changed so much for humans that his story is a shadow of what is possible for many people. And, more importantly, how it could be possible for you.

I've divided the book into four parts to clearly outline the journey. In Part One, I'll talk about why it's so important for you to make a change, and how Happy High Achievers hit similar markers or milestones along the way. I'll also look at the biggest obstacles that might be stopping you from finding fulfilling work.

In Part Two, I'll prepare you for your career-change journey. If you want to do something that most consider impossible, you'll need a different level of preparation. This includes deciphering how top performers build a profile of their ideal career by considering and exploring the seven key elements that bring fulfillment to any career, which I'll discuss in Part Three.

Part Four is all about the doing, the landing, and the thriving, beginning with designing experiments, adjusting when things don't work out as you imagined, and then learning how to thrive—which, as it turns out, is far different from just showing up to your ideal situation and expecting it to be rainbows and butterflies.

Most people don't even realize career change is possible, or they feel stuck. But as I have worked with our clients over the last decade and helped thousands of people make career changes to fulfilling work that also pays well, I've learned that you need to see for yourself that it's real. Once you see what's possible, it's almost impossible not to change your mindset, and that's exactly what you need to do to make career change happen. This is why you'll find a list of resources at the end of the book that includes links to podcast episodes for almost every story I've included. These are stories of real people sharing in their own words how they made incredible career changes to much more fulfilling work.

It doesn't matter where you're starting from; what matters is that you're making the choice now to do things drastically differently going forward. You can live and work intentionally. And I will show you that career change is far more than simply changing companies.

Even if you have already decided that change is for you, one thing I've learned in studying human psychology, behavior, and, ultimately, career success is there is no one set of steps. We all have different road maps and ladders, and anyone who tells you differently is full of it. This is why this change is so hard. That's not to say that there are no commonalities among Happy High Achievers and their journeys. There are similar milestones they all hit along the way. And that's what I'd like to talk about next.

Happen To Checklist

Take some time to think about your answers to these questions to determine if a career change is right for you right now:

☐ If you're still in the same place twelve months from now, is that good for you?

☐ How are other people in your life affected if you don't change?

☐ What's the worst thing that could happen if you change? If you don't change?

☐ Are you actively setting yourself up (now) for the life you want to live later? What would that look like?

☐ What is your current path if you don't intervene? Are you okay with that?

☐ Are there any pieces of your current situation that you're tolerating right now? What are you willing to do to change that?

2

Happy High Achiever Milestones

It had long since come to my attention that people
of accomplishment rarely sat back and let things happen
to them. They went out and happened to things."

**ATTRIBUTED TO ANDREA DEL VERROCCHIO
(DA VINCI'S MENTOR)**

"I COULD FEEL myself coming alive."

That's what Stephanie Bilbrey told me when she got a small first taste of what work could be like when her personal needs were aligned with her career pursuits. Stephanie didn't quite believe it was possible . . . until it happened.

Life is very different for Stephanie, who is now working as a content and communications strategist in a company that she loves and believes in. Yes, she's much happier with her work, but it's much more than that. She described her work to me as when you "get to do what you can't stop doing." Imagine that! Getting paid for what you can't help yourself from doing and thinking about anyway, in a company that values your contribution and experience, and surrounded by other people who are just as excited about what you're accomplishing as you are. Oh, and the kicker? What if you got paid more for this new, heightened quality of life? Stephanie was talking to me from a house that she had purchased as a result of her career change, which nearly doubled her salary. Best of all, Stephanie was in her element after spending over sixteen years working in roles that were good, but just didn't quite fit.

Soon after Stephanie became an event manager, a moment involving a highly agitated client (who was upset that the napkins were off-white instead of white) made her realize the role was not a good fit. In fact, she had never quite had a job that truly fit. Over the next ten years she tried working in marketing, moved across the country, and even dabbled in higher education. You have to give her credit; she wasn't about to accept work that wasn't working! After all these years of trying solutions and thinking, This will be it, she'd finally concluded that she needed a complete overhaul in her approach to finding work that fit her priorities. It was only after she made the decision to go all-in on her self-development that she began to recognize what she truly wanted and needed to thrive.

Stephanie began journaling and listening to the *Happen to Your Career Podcast*. After she reached out to us, we started working with her to get her prepared for a successful career change. We then took her through the process of career change, which resulted in not just one but multiple offers that fit her ideal version of work.

The great news is that Happy High Achievers all journey through the same four major milestones. Navigating through each of these milestones allows you to see how a path to a change to fulfilling work is possible. Still, it's critical to be aware that everyone will reach the milestones in slightly (sometimes drastically) different ways. Everyone crosses the same bridges, but in their own way.

Also crucial to know is that working through these milestones may take different amounts of time. Most people we work with at HTYC take six to eighteen months to make a career change. You will have your own time schedule, but the milestones are the same for everyone.

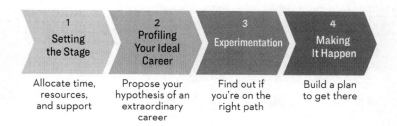

1 Setting the Stage	2 Profiling Your Ideal Career	3 Experimentation	4 Making It Happen
Allocate time, resources, and support	Propose your hypothesis of an extraordinary career	Find out if you're on the right path	Build a plan to get there

Setting the Stage

The first milestone is setting up your life to temporarily make career change a priority. This includes allocating the appropriate time and resources so you can work on your change. But it also includes building the right support team and even getting your life, relationships, and skills to the point where it is easier to change careers.

Profiling Your Ideal Career

Next, you need to create a hypothesis about what an extraordinary career means for you. Scientific research can inform you about some critical elements you need in your career, but it's up to you to prioritize these elements and declare your own version of ideal.

Experimentation

The next milestone involves validating your new direction before you do the work to get there. You have a hypothesis about what you want; now you need to design some career experiments to find out if you're on the right path. In the process, you might also learn what you don't want or what is not acceptable for you in a new role, so this milestone includes adjusting and tweaking your hypothesis of your ideal career.

Making It Happen

Once you know where you're going, you can build a plan to get there. The benefit to knowing what you want is that you can ask for it. But career change is not over once you've arrived in your new role. You'll need to learn to behave differently to fully enjoy the benefits of the work you've done on changing your career and aligning it with your life.

THROUGHOUT THE book I will offer examples of how people have moved through the milestones. My intent is that by the end of the book you will be able to say, "I see how this could work for me." Along the way, I will show you what life might be like for you once you make a career change, but I'll also be honest about the challenges that may face you in your journey to becoming a Happy High Achiever.

Happy High Achievers are people who are successful in their work and life in ways they have defined personally, without achieving that success at the expense of everything else in their lives. For Stephanie, becoming a Happy High Achiever meant finding the feeling of "I get to do this" in her work and being compensated well for it. For Michael, the former finance executive, it meant finding work that allowed him to use his strengths and natural inclinations; work that could actually be fun and that allowed him to be flexible, to take care of himself, and to be truly healthy.

Becoming a Happy High Achiever means something different for everyone. Maybe it's about being able to live out your creative dreams while still getting paid a premium. Maybe it's about doing work you find more meaningful. Maybe it's about being able to be there for your family, kids, or significant other while contributing to the world because you just can't stop thinking about the future and what could be possible . . . okay, maybe that one is me.

The point is that if you want it to be, your quality of life can be immensely better than it is right now. Doing work that fits with who you are, who you want to be, and the life you want to live makes it so. Finding this kind of work doesn't mean everything is perfect or without challenges. But it does mean that you get to be you. And it does mean that you feel meaning and purpose, and that you're spending your time contributing in a way that you can't help but want to contribute already. It's a different way to operate. Every single person I've talked to who is in the Happy High Achievers' club has told me they couldn't go back to doing work and life the old way.

Of course, this doesn't mean career change is easy. There are many reasons people are stopped in their tracks and never make the change. The biggest problem is that they are not the obvious reasons. What if the real things stopping you from finding fulfilling work were those you couldn't even see?

In the next chapter, I'll introduce you to the hidden obstacles that might stop you. More importantly, I'll discuss how some of these are the same problems that restaurants, Jeff Bezos, and even Alice faced during her time in Wonderland!

Happen To Checklist

Answer these questions:

☐ Which Happy High Achiever milestone do you believe will be the most challenging for you? Why?

☐ What can you do right now to move past this obstacle?

Happen To Bonus

Learn how unconventional career change might be possible for you. Visit happentoyourcareer.com/bonus for a list of the stories in this book. Pick one and find out how that person made their career change.

3

The Five Hidden Obstacles to Change

The only use of an obstacle is to be overcome.
WOODROW WILSON

FOR MORE than eight years, Jenny had proudly told others she was a research scientist. In many ways this had been part of her identity from an early age because she'd grown up in a family of scientists and academics. No surprise, then, that when Jenny became an adult, she devoted fifteen years to developing her skills and expertise to earn her position. Her role as a research scientist was prestigious, stable, and well paid, in a location that she and her family loved.

Although this may sound like a Netflix-worthy "work-hard" story in which the main character achieves a much-desired life goal, it's not the whole story. Despite her achievement, Jenny began to realize in the first few years of her research role that something wasn't right. Science she loved; but the specifics of her position, not so much! As much as Jenny appreciated and wanted to love her job, it was the wrong fit. Collaboration, outreach, and mentoring younger scientists—the things that made science engaging for Jenny—were not rewarded as much as individual achievements and fast-paced production of research papers. Very few of her strengths were reflected in the metrics by which she was evaluated, something she hadn't anticipated in advance. Requests for a flexible schedule when her two kids were babies could not be granted. Over time, the mismatches made her anxious and miserable and began to affect her family. Still, it took Jenny over three years to leave her job. Why?

What I've learned is that Jenny's experience (like that of Michael, whom we met earlier) is not only common but also typical. In the work my team and I do at HTYC, we see this same phenomenon every day. This inability to move out of one role to another that is more fulfilling does raise a bigger set of questions:

- Why do smart, capable people struggle to change careers?

- What is the reason people like Jenny and Michael might wait months or years before they do anything about it?

- When they finally do decide they need to make a change, what stops them from finding work that fits?

- What can high performers like Jenny *do* about it?

I will tease apart the answers to that last question throughout the rest of this book. But to answer the other questions, you must understand the critical reasons that stop top performers from making a career change. I say "critical" reasons because there are many more than I can discuss in this book, so I will focus on the most common and highest-impact reasons that people get stopped in their career-change tracks before they ever start.

Jenny did transition eventually into a new career that she loves, but only after many false starts and setbacks in her job search. Almost all high-performing people who change careers must overcome the same obstacles that Jenny did. These break down into what I call the Five Obstacles of Career Change, and each of these has a certain kind of mindset attached to it. See if you recognize yourself in any of these thought patterns:

* "I've worked hard to get where I am, and I don't want to lose what I have. I'm more worried about losing what I have than I am excited about what I might gain."

* "I'm not spending enough time with my family as it is, and even if I were to make a change, I just feel drained from my job."

* "I don't know what else is out there for me and I don't know how to look for it."

* "My parents always expected me to do this work. Besides, everyone is telling me that I should just stick it out because I have a good situation."

* "I don't know where I'm running to, so what's the point of doing all this work?"

The purpose of this chapter is to allow you to recognize when you're facing any or all five obstacles. You have to be able to recognize what's happening before you can do anything about it. Ready for some self-revelation?

The Monkey with a Hand Stuck in the Jar

Kim was a government employee earning about $120,000 per year doing project management. She stayed in her job because she didn't want to quit for one reason. Any guesses as to what it was?

Kim (whose name isn't really Kim, but let's protect the innocent) told me that she had once loved her job, but that was no longer the case. Now she was bored and found the work to be drudgery. Did she love working for the government? No, not at all. She was tired of the bureaucracy and the lack of tangible impact of her work. Was it the people, then? Still nope.

So why did she stay? Well, what's the one great thing all government jobs have? You guessed it: great benefits. Loss aversion, or when you get your hand stuck in a jar, is an obstacle many people stumble over as they consider making a career change. In Kim's case, she was reluctant to give up her benefits.

Now, in a former career, I was an HR director responsible for purchasing benefits for entire organizations of employees. From my vantage point, Kim's benefits weren't that lucrative. I figured they were worth about $15,000 per year. Translation: If she found a new job that paid her $15,000 more than her current salary—a totally reasonable 12.5% raise—she could purchase her own benefits *and* have a job she enjoyed. Yet the so-called security of having those benefits was holding her back. Three years after our phone call, Kim was still stuck in the same job and still unhappy, trapped in government-benefit golden handcuffs.

What's going on here?

It's similar to the story of the monkey who reaches his hand into a jar because he sees a banana. Once he clamps his hand around the banana, he can't get it out of the jar. The thought of letting go of the banana never enters his mind, so he stays with one hand stuck inside the jar.

We humans are influenced far more by avoiding loss than we are by pursuing gains. Nobel Prize–winner Daniel Kahneman illustrated this in a study in which he performed experiments with participants who reported their feelings about gaining or losing the same amount of money.[1] The distress participants reported over losing some money was far greater than the joy or happiness that accompanied gaining the same amount of money. Think about it this way: participants were far more upset about losing $200 than they were excited about gaining $200.

But loss aversion isn't just about money. Potential losses in all areas of life have an impact on our choices without us even realizing it, even if those losses aren't real or are highly unlikely. Worse, we (myself included) believe that we're being completely rational, reasonable, and logical in how we perceive, anticipate, and behave about potential losses. Worse still, loss aversion prevents us (especially high performers) from getting to a point where we are thriving in our careers.

I don't want to lose what I have. This is the lament of every person who refuses to leave an unfulfilling job, a company that they've outgrown, or a role that no longer fits them even if it's making them miserable. I know this is true because at HTYC we have collected well over three thousand responses from high performers who are on the cusp of career change. Here's how this loss aversion shows up in their words:

* "I don't want to give up the flexibility I have."

* "I'm worried that I won't be able to make as much money doing something else."

* "I have great benefits. I don't want to lose those."

* "I work with great people. I'm not sure If I'll be able to find that anyplace else."

* "I've worked really hard to get my degrees. I don't want to start over."

High-achieving, talented people ignore the possibility of something far better than they can even imagine because they're scared of what they might lose by leaving their current job. Let me be clear: If you want to retain your flexibility, it's absolutely possible. Want to work with a talented supportive team? You can. Want to retain your current salary and lifestyle? Awesome!

Changing organizations or jobs is usually the best time to get a raise because that's when you have the most bargaining power. As I will discuss in Chapter 4, the best way to think about career change is as an opportunity to carry over what you have already and fill in the gaps from your current situation. Out of the several thousands of people my company has worked with during their career changes, we've rarely found any who needed to give up or lose anything.

Jenny, our research scientist, experienced this phenomenon of loss aversion deeply. You sense that fear of loss vibrating through her story. She started to feel unhappy in her job, and her mind immediately turned against her, resistant, refusing to move forward. She eventually began to recognize this for what it was: an obstacle on the path to career change, holding her back.

Spoiler alert: Jenny did transition. She didn't give up everything, still made great money, and found a role that was a much better fit for her. One where she got to share her love of science but not the research that she intensely disliked.

When you're not moving forward because you fear potentially losing something, that is a red flag. But you can learn from the stories of Jenny and Kim and see that this obstacle is more illusion than fact. Unfortunately, this human tendency to avoid loss also works hand in hand with the next obstacle.

The Merry-Go-Round of Repetitive Despair

Have you ever heard of the "experience catch-22" that so often plagues young job seekers stuck in entry-level roles? It goes like this: all the jobs require experience, but you have to get the job to get the experience. Well, it turns out that career change, even for those with plenty of work experience, has its own special breed of catch-22: a perpetual lack of energy and time.

This is a direct path to the merry-go-round of repetitive despair. The song played over and over on this particular merry-go-round is, "All my time and energy are consumed by the job I no longer want, so I can't make time to do anything about it, so I guess I stay." Catchy tune, right?

Here's how my team and I have heard this paradox show up when we talk with people who want to make career changes: "When I get home from work, it's all I can do to just make dinner. Then, on the weekends, I'm just so drained that by the time I recover, it's Monday again. I simply don't have the energy to do the work to make a career change."

If you're giving your current role everything that you have to give and then are depleted at the end of your workdays and weekends, it's no surprise that making a large life change is going to be extra challenging. But this particular obstacle is far more devious than that. It's not so much the lack of energy that is the obstacle. It's that many would-be career changers *think* it's an obstacle.

Here's what I mean. Most people who've had any career success got there by working hard. Working hard usually also means working a lot of hours. This isn't a completely bad situation by itself, but when that same person thinks about career change, they may feel depressed and hopeless. They may ask themselves, "How am I going to find the time to figure out how to make a career change? I'm barely fitting in all the hours as it is!"

What's even more troublesome about this tune is that it may convince you that job situations that appear out of the blue were "meant to be." For example, perhaps you receive an email from a friend who's starting a new department and who asks if you will come work for them even though you have to take a salary cut and travel extensively for the first six months. Let's say one of the reasons you want to get away from your current role in the first place is to spend more time with your family. But now you might be trying to convince yourself that six months of traveling is a minor inconvenience because surely it will get better if you give it a little time. It's a small price to pay to get away from the job you are in, right?

Everyone has heard someone tell them, "Give it a little time." This is the common cure-all, so much so that we may focus on it intensely on as the solution for everything.

- I just need more time . . .
- When I find the time . . .
- If only I had time . . .

Giving it a little time is a great solution, but only if you want to work yourself into the ground while surrounded by many other miserable people watching you do it.

One person who seems adept at bending time to his will is Jeff Bezos, the founder and former CEO of Amazon. When Jeff Bezos was CEO, he used to take big-decision meetings only between 10 am and lunchtime.[2] Whether you believe Amazon is the best company in the world or a dismal place to be, we can agree that they accomplish the previously impossible at record-breaking speeds. How do they do that? Did Jeff Bezos invent the thirty-two-hour day? Is Amazon manufacturing extra hours that they give to their employees? Do they issue time-turners on orientation day, like Hermione used at Hogwarts? No, no, and no.

Over the years, I've gained a lot of insight into Amazon. Our HTYC team has helped many people transition into or out of Amazon. I've been recruited by Amazon many times over the years. My brother-in-law and good friends work for Amazon. This has given me the opportunity to study the organization from multiple angles. I believe the reason Amazon is so effective as a company is that they focus on strategic action and *not* on time. Amazon makes small bets initially and tests them before going all in—strategic action after strategic action, over and over again.

So, how does this apply to career change? What stops so many people from taking real steps toward fulfilling work that also pays well is their focus on a *perceived* lack of time and energy. But when you've been successful in the past by working harder and longer than everyone else, or by being willing to do more than everyone else, it can be hard to switch gears. If you want to become a Happy High Achiever, you will need to learn how to do things differently.

So, hear me now: your new mantra is *effective action*, not time.

Let's agree that even though working hard and for long hours has served you in the past, it is not going to help you make that career change to become a Happy High Achiever. And this leads us right into the next obstacle.

The Restaurant with No Menus

Imagine that you've walked into a restaurant you've never dined in before. The maître d' seats you, and everything appears normal. But then you discover that there are no menus, chalk boards on the wall, or any other presented options or specials. You're feeling adventurous, so you decide to roll with it, and then the waiter comes back and asks, "What do you want? We can make you anything!"

Anything? Um . . . okay . . .

Restaurants would never do this because it would kill sales. Why? Two reasons.

First, it's far too difficult for customers to make a decision when there are no options to consider. It's far easier for the customer to point to a menu and say, "I would like the nine-layer dip, please!" It's even better if there is a picture of the nine-layer dip on the menu, because then they can imagine what it might taste like and decide whether they want it. Second, it's impossible to order dishes that you've never heard of, even if the restaurant can make them.

The crazy thing is that this is *exactly* the problem you're facing this very moment.

Since you've made it this far into the book, you already suspect you need to make a change. Although your intuition about this is likely correct, your next question is probably, A change to what? You don't know what your options are if you don't know they exist.

Jenny and Kim both suffered from a lack of exposure to the career options that were available to them. Once they were ready to consider moving on from their unhappy but well-paid roles, they had no idea what to do next or how to look for it. More significant is that they had no idea what was truly possible for them.

Let's go back to a restaurant for a moment, but one that does have a menu. If you're like me, you might seriously deliberate over whether you're going to choose between the raspberry cheesecake and the Italian doughnuts with little dipping sauces. (Seriously, I might regret not ordering the cheesecake, but Alyssa frowns on me pulling out a spreadsheet to do a "regret" analysis during date night.) Yes, this is an obviously massive problem (especially if the doughnuts are amazing), but at least you have specific choices in front of you.

In life, and especially in careers, this is not the case. Many high achievers can do many things, and there are many ways they can achieve their career goals. The only thing limiting them is what they've seen or witnessed before. Or, to keep running with the restaurant analogy, we order off the only menu we can see in front of us.

For example, when I was in college, I owned a painting business for three years that paid for my wife's engagement ring and almost all my college tuition and expenses. At the height of my business, I had twenty-five people working for me and it was really profitable (after I learned how to run a business solidly... my sincere apologies to the homeowners I worked with in my first year!). But when I graduated from college, I sold my business and took a corporate job that I was not excited about, where I worked eighty to ninety hours a week for less money.

Why on earth would I do this?

Well, I traded a desirable situation for a horrible one because I didn't know that being a business owner was a viable career option. I know that sounds absurd, but here's what played into that decision. When I was growing up, my family was poor. At one point we existed on food stamps, and my mom still tells me stories about writing checks that she desperately hoped would clear the bank. I didn't want to live like that ever again. I thought that what you did to avoid poverty was go to college, get good grades, get a good job, work your way up the ladder quickly, and make tons of money, so I could have all the things I didn't have growing up. I thought that would make me happy.

Yes, I know that sounds even more absurd. But stay with me for a second.

The only people I knew who owned businesses were struggling, at best. In my mind, business owner equated with poor, struggling, and unhappy. There were no happy, thriving business owners on my menu, so instead I ordered what I saw on my personal menu in front of me. Hello mediocre job that paid me less! I simply didn't understand that you could be a happy business owner because I had never been exposed to the possibility.

Lack of exposure to what's possible, and how it could be possible for you, is one of the principal places where people get stuck. It creates blinders even in places where you don't realize there could be blinders. Often you're convinced you don't have blinders until they are removed. This is one of the reasons my company has produced a weekly podcast since 2013 that showcases stories of high achievers who've made seemingly impossible career changes. It exposes would-be career changers to what is possible. The more exposure you have to what's possible, the more options you can see on your personal career menu.

So, get that menu ready. I just decided I'm ordering the doughnuts *and* the cheesecake.

The Should Factor

The expectations of others who tell you what you should or should not do in your career is a wall you will need to climb repeatedly as you work through a career change. "Should" is a four-letter word if your goal is thriving in your career or any area of your life. To see how the should factor works against you as an obstacle, let's go back to Jenny, our reluctant research scientist.

Here's what was going on in Jenny's head at the time she was thinking about making a career change. She had been offered the opportunity that countless women in science had never received, and now she was going to . . . throw it away? Wouldn't this demonstrate that women couldn't hack it in the lab? She had been allowed to stay when other people on her research team had been laid off because of budget cuts. Now here she was considering quitting. Wasn't this disrespectful of the people who had lost their jobs?

As she thought about these things, Jenny went through all the feels. She felt sick. She felt like a bad person. At times she felt miserable. But what was common among all of these thoughts keeping Jenny in the job? They were all things Jenny thought she "should" do because of what she believed others expected from her.

Jenny tried to fight through the expectations of others. She told me that her mindset was, "I need to just perform better. I need to put my blinders on and, no excuses, get better at the areas that I'm not strong in." Still, Jenny couldn't fight the feeling that her research job was just not a fit for her. She loved working with other people, but research science isn't so much about that. It's about publishing: do the research, write papers, get published—that's the job. Jenny could do that; she just didn't enjoy it. Over time, she realized she wanted to help contribute to science in a very different way. And she realized that rather than brutalizing herself about improving her weaknesses, she would be better off finding another job that catered to her strengths.

As I have studied high achievers and top performers over the years, I've seen that each of them had to find the path that worked for them. In this case, finding your own path means learning to ignore the "shoulds" and instead focus on what is good for you.

The first step is to recognize when you're getting "should on" by well-meaning people. And then when you're doing it to yourself. This may sound crazy, but this awareness is a skill that can be developed. You can learn to recognize when you're going up against yourself. Much like everything else, you will have to experiment and learn what is right for you. Let me explore three common examples of when the should factor shows up most often.

Career Advice

I can't tell you the number of times I've heard, "Well, I talked to a recruiter about my situation, and they said [insert what you might want here, and then let the recruiter rip any shred of hope about that away from you]."

People are quick to tell you what you should do, but they don't often consider whether their advice fits *you*. Whether the person delivering advice is your boss, mentor, friends, family, or coworkers, all of them are looking at your situation through their own lens. And they all have their own version of the exposure problem going on; they only have their own menu. Here's what that sounds like:

- "There will always be a need for [insert occupation of choice], so that would be a great profession for you."

- "There are no perfect jobs, so I think you should just keep pushing through."

- "What about your bonus next year? You should at least stay until then."

- "You're so great at your job! Why would you want to quit?"

No matter how well meaning, these advisors are not you. What they want, what they would do, is not the same for you. Filter their advice through this lens. Some of the best advice I receive comes in the form of great questions that force me to decide for myself.

The Needs of Family and Loved Ones

This is a huge obstacle, because career change for you so often means big changes for your family and those you care about. You might find yourself thinking and worrying along these lines:

- "I should keep this job to provide for my family. After all, my kids are almost in college. After that, I can focus on me."

- "I should just keep pushing through because I don't want my wife to have all the extra stress of a career change."

That second example is a personal "should" from my past. But I was already causing extra stress by bringing my misery home in the evenings. When staying in place for family reasons affects the greater good of your family, continuing on that same path becomes less noble or useful. Is it a good thing if the college is paid for but you've taught your kid that you have to put up with work that's making you miserable to do so? If you stay in place, your partner doesn't have to face the stress of a career change for several months, but they still need to deal with the stress of you being in a bad mood constantly because you dislike your job.

Only you can decide if the actual tradeoffs are right for you, but most of the people we've worked with at HTYC have found that with a few conversations (and some proactivity), they can avoid most of the potential negatives. We will discuss how to address expectations of family in the chapter on planning for inevitable success, Chapter 5. In the meantime, don't allow your well-meaning intention to do the "thing you should do" for your family to stop you from doing the things that are right for them in the long term.

Job Search Methods

Do any of these quotes reflect what is going on with you right now?

- "I've done a few informational interviews, but it hasn't panned out."

- "I've been told I should update my LinkedIn profile, but honestly, I don't really want to spend a lot of time on LinkedIn."

- "Either all the job postings I find sound terrible or the couple I've been interested in want years of experience."

When people approach career change, many assume they're only qualified to do the same work they've been doing. So, when they contemplate moving into another industry, the first thing they do is look at job boards: "Maybe I could be a [insert your thing here]. Let's see who's hiring for that." What they find is a limited number of jobs narrowly tailored to people with specific skills and experience levels that the companies believe they want for the positions. The odds are that career-change seekers don't have all the necessary skills or experiences that match these job descriptions because they're currently working in a different industry. Too often, as a result, people conclude that career change is impossible and give up.

The Cheshire Cat

"Would you tell me, please, which way I ought to go from here?"

"That depends a good deal on where you want to get to," said the Cat.

"I don't much care where—" said Alice.

"Then it doesn't much matter which way you go," said the Cat.

LEWIS CARROLL, *Alice's Adventures in Wonderland*

Before I was a career coach, I worked in human resources, which meant I had to read a ton of resumes and conduct a lot of interviews. I'll be honest: I got bored, because all the resumes and interviews were the same. After a while, I began looking for a way to get some different answers out of interview candidates, something more insightful and honest than the usual "please hire me, I promise I'm normal" job interview script. What I finally hit on was a simple series of questions.

First, I would ask interviewees what they hoped to gain from the job they were interviewing for. Almost everyone gave the same answer: "Growth." My deceptively simple follow-up question was, "What does growth mean for you?" This never struck me as a difficult question, but almost no one could answer it. They wanted "growth," but they had no idea what that meant. Did they want more money, more responsibility, more training? They didn't know.

Now for the third question: What was it about their prior job that had prompted them to seek a new job? Almost everyone could answer this one. Most people had a litany of complaints, a parade of outrages, that they had suffered at their previous job and did not want to have happen again at their new job.

I asked these three questions of hundreds of job applicants until the pattern was clear. When it came to looking for a job, almost everyone knew what they were running from, but almost no one knew what they were running to. Almost no one knew what they wanted. It didn't matter where they went, because it didn't seem to matter where they wanted to go.

The other thing I learned from these questions was the power of clarity. When I did interview someone who truly knew what they wanted from the job, who knew what they were running to, not just what they were running from, that person almost always got a job offer. Our research scientist Jenny is a good example. She was unable to move her career change forward until she knew what she wanted. When a person has the strength of character to know what they want and to go after it, other people will rally around that person.

Once you can identify what you want—what you are running to, not just what you are running from—you will find that people from your friends and loved ones to complete strangers to large organizations will go out of their way to help you achieve it.

THE FIVE hidden obstacles we've covered in this chapter will pop up when you least expect. Your first line of defense is being aware they even exist. Your many potential backup lines of defense will be covered in Chapter 5. First, though, you need to know what lessons Google Maps can teach about how to make yourself exempt from job qualifications and conventional hiring black holes. And, most importantly, how to avoid ending up outside in the middle of winter in just your t-shirt.

Happen To Checklist

Answer these questions:

- [ ] What are the losses you're trying to avoid?
- [ ] How can you expose yourself to what might be possible for you?
- [ ] What expectations from others might be stopping you from moving forward?

Happen To Bonus

Which of the five obstacles is most likely to have an impact on your career change? What's one small thing you can do about it? If you're not sure, you can always schedule a conversation with the team at HTYC to find the help you need by going to happentoyourcareer.com/schedule.

PART TWO

PREPARING FOR THE JOURNEY

4

Begin with the End

Recast your current problems into proactive goals.
SUZE ORMAN

REMEMBER THE moment that changed my career philosophy forever.

I was faced with a terrifying, life-altering decision. Years of hard work and career advancement lay behind me, and a bright and lucrative future lay ahead. All I had to do was answer one simple question. But I was stumped. Alyssa, my wife, was trying to help me, but she was stumped, too. At first glance, the answer appeared simple enough. But the more we thought about it, the more confusing it became, like a finger trap for our brains. Finally, we were out of time. We had to decide.

Did we want to move to Omaha, Nebraska, or not?

At the time I was working in human resources for a Fortune 500 company. Alyssa and I were living happily in Washington State, where we intended to raise our kids. I was on the VP track at work. But to reach the VP level, the company wanted me to work in the Omaha office for a few years. They flew me and Alyssa to Nebraska and showed us the best that Omaha has to offer. We were impressed! We were wined and dined and taken to some NCAA tournament games. We looked at some potential houses, and then we flew back home.

After we returned, Alyssa and I found ourselves standing on opposite sides of the island in our kitchen, debriefing each other about the trip so we could make a final decision. We were doing this, right? I was going to be a VP. We were moving to Nebraska. There would probably be fewer Starbucks and more steak in our future. Right?

But then Alyssa asked me about what we would do after we got back to Washington. And as we started talking about that, it hit me. If Washington State was where we wanted to be, then why would we leave? Come to think of it, why did I want to be a VP? I mean, VP of what? The company said we would figure that out in a few years. That's a vague prospect to plan your future around. And what was the point of becoming a VP? More money? We were already financially comfortable. We didn't need to uproot our whole lives and move away from a place we loved just to get more money.

Eventually, we framed the discussion this way: What was our end goal? What did we want our lives to look like, and how would my next career move fit into that plan? If our goal was to live and raise a family in Washington, then moving to Nebraska seemed like a step in the wrong direction. I decided to turn down any opportunities in Omaha. And Alyssa and I decided to stay in Moses Lake, Washington, where we still live with our three children.

Through this journey I learned an essential truth about career change: that an ideal career and an ideal life are mutually dependent. Don't believe me? Think about any other area of your life:

- Time with your partner or family depends on your work schedule and what's acceptable.

- Accomplishing your financial goals depends on your income, especially if most or all of your income is related to your work. Choosing to spend time in one opportunity versus another means you might be restricting your ability to meet your financial goals.

- How you dress and the clothes you choose to buy depend on what is socially acceptable at your work and whom you spend the most time with.[1]

- Even how much you smile per day depends on your work. People who spend more time working in areas where they are strong and capable smile more times per day.[2]

Conversely, your work is also dependent on your life circumstances. For example:

- If your spouse or partner isn't supportive of you changing careers, HTYC experience shows that your desired career change is less likely to happen.

- If you're in poor health or not getting sleep, it's going to impact your performance at work.

- If you aren't making enough money to pay your bills, good luck trying to be fully productive.

- Even if you are making enough money to pay your bills, likely you have adjusted your lifestyle and goals to need a higher level of income. That means you may not be willing to do work that pays any amount, no matter how rewarding.

So, let's stop pretending life and work are separate. They aren't. They are mutually dependent. Making this one change in your mindset will lead you to the next step, which is all about knowing and understanding where you want to get to.

What this means is that if you want to find your version of your ideal career, you have to know what you want your ideal life to look like. One will not happen without the other. In my experience, people who are thriving in career and life are not doing this by accident. Instead they carefully evaluate what is most important to them in their work and life circumstances and recognize that this will change over time. What if you were to begin with the end in mind and use that to inform not only what job you want, but how you go about getting it?

Avoid the Road Trip to Nowhere

Over the years, I've received thousands of emails from people all over the world—high-performing, successful people—who feel as if they have no control over the course of their career. They've moved from role to role, or organization to organization, almost randomly. A boss offered them a promotion, so they took it. A recruiter contacted them and said they might be a good fit for another position, so they pursued it. A friend called and said they would be perfect for a job. These career changes may have been an improvement compared to the old job, but it's far from intentional, just as the potential move to Omaha was for me and Alyssa. We realized that going to Omaha would take us away from our end goal to live and raise our family in Washington.

When you know the end goal, the steps along the way will become much clearer. Like taking a road trip, if you don't know where you're going, then you might end up somewhere you aren't all that happy about. You might end up in Great Falls, Montana, in the middle of winter with snow blowing around at minus fifteen degrees Fahrenheit. Okay, yes, you lived some wild moments along the way, like almost crashing along Lookout Pass and buying beef jerky at midnight at a sketchy gas station because you ran out of snacks. But now you're in Montana... without a warm coat.

Instead, if you know that you want to go to Tallahassee, Florida, where it's nice and warm, you can punch Tallahassee into the GPS and figure out the route you want to take. You can pack for the weather and even figure out what you want to do in Florida before you arrive.

When you begin with the end in mind, you know where you are running to as well as where you are running from. The magic of defining your destination is that it's radically different from the way most people approach their career change. And it turns out that when you take a radically different approach, you can achieve radically different results.

Pursue the Unconventional

Just before I wrote this chapter, I had a call with Larry, who was accepted to a certification program that he technically (and un-technically) did not qualify for. The certifying organization had previously told him no, he must have certain qualifications to "get in." However, Larry received an exception from these qualifications because he was willing to persist even though his background and expertise were vastly different from the normal requirements (there's that "normal" word again!). How? He got to know the people in the certifying organization and was able to get an exception because of his unique experience.

Larry had industry experience that nobody else with the certification had. As he interacted with the people in charge of the certification, they saw the benefit of his industry knowledge. Larry didn't let the listed qualifications dictate whether he was qualified for the program. That's a simple example of taking an unconventional approach.

Here are some other examples of real people HTYC has worked with who've taken some unusual approaches to finding new careers. Each of these approaches seems unconventional, but they were all successful at opening doors for the career-change seekers.

- Eric contacted CEOs, directors, and engineers at different companies for the purpose of getting their comments on a blog post he was writing about their industry (even though he wasn't a writer by trade).

- Mike set up an entire day of casual conversations at five different companies that he was interested in working with and learned all about the challenges they were facing. After the conversations, Mike worked up some solutions for these challenges for free (and without the companies knowing) and presented them a week later to the respective organizations.

- Kristy worked with the president of a company to create a role that was literally made for her. She had done a small amount of side work for the company previously and identified a need for the organization. When she approached the owner to find out if he saw the same need, this led to a series of conversations and an opportunity for which Kristy was the only considered candidate. This initial opportunity ultimately became the stepping stone to Kristy's full-time career in the industry she most wanted to be a part of—the wine and travel industry.

Larry, Eric, Mike, and Kristy all had something in common: they pursued unicorn-level opportunities and got results. In other words, they looked for opportunities that are supposed to be impossible and that many people don't believe exist.

To find the impossible, you must be willing to do the work that gets exceptions made for you, as well as knowing where you want to run to. This is definitely a challenge! But you are a high performer, right? So, let's assume you're willing to do unconventional work to get unconventional results. That doesn't mean that you should do this haphazardly.

Treat it Like a Puzzle

Ever seen a toddler do a puzzle? They just start grabbing random pieces and seeing if they fit together. These two? No. These two? No. Then they get frustrated, leading to the inevitable, "I can't do it!" Tears, throwing pieces, punching the floor. That's what was happening with my son Grayson when he was three years old. Only the sounds he was making made me confused about whether he was frustrated or constipated.

I decided that since he was still mashing pieces together unsuccessfully, it was probably puzzle frustration. So I sat down with him on the floor to show him how to make building a puzzle so much easier than jamming each individual piece against another piece. The trick is to start the puzzle by finding the corner pieces, then finding the edge pieces, then assembling the edges into a complete frame. Only then does it become much easier to see what the picture might be.

As I helped Grayson build that puzzle, I realized many of us are experiencing the same frustration with our careers. We change jobs and think, That's the piece that will work. Nope. We accept a promotion or get recruited for a role. Nope, still doesn't fit. We think, If only I was making more money, or in the tech industry, or didn't have to travel so much, or [fill in the blank], then things would come together. Eventually we don't even know where to begin because we can't see how the pieces could go together. So we give up.

But what if we approached our careers strategically, the same way we might do a puzzle?

When a Good Job is Not a Great Fit

Let's pretend you've done all the hard work of applying for a job. You've made it to the final round of interviews. You're elated because the role is everything you hoped for. The organization offers you the position, and you accept it and realize how fortunate you are to have been given this chance. Weeks later, reality crashes down. Everything you were looking forward to is not a part of the job. Nothing at all.

This is what happened to Cheri Thom when she started her new role at a large healthcare entity. She told me, "I had been a business analyst for quite a long time prior to starting... I spent time with the customers, I worked with them to figure out what they wanted to do with their tools to make their jobs more efficient or add functionality or whatever it was. So when I was going into this role, that was what I expected."

Instead, Cheri was spending all her time reading documentation, and she had little to no interaction with people. "I was missing the entire social aspect of why I got into business analysis in the first place. So that was a huge mess. And I didn't like their management style." Cheri hadn't thought about where she wanted to end up, and she didn't realize that until she found herself in a job where she knew she didn't belong.

So she started doing what anyone would do: she turned to online job postings and started applying like mad to get out. Unfortunately, this tried and not-so-true tactic isn't particularly useful when you haven't spent the time to define what you want. Why? Because it almost always leads you to a variation of the same place you're at. Kind of like finding a piece of the puzzle that's the right colour but not the right shape.

Cheri confirmed, "For a long time I was applying for anything that fit within the realm of possibility because I wanted out. And obviously that was probably not going to work out in my favor, long term." Sadly, things only got worse for Cheri.

Almost everyone I've encountered through my years of career coaching underestimates the impact that even a "good job" that isn't a fit is having on their lives. In Cheri's case, her role was not a fit at all, and it was having far-reaching consequences that she didn't anticipate. The terrible experience she was having was causing her to question everything. "I felt like I couldn't trust myself, and I didn't know what I wanted to do. I had been happy in my previous role, but I got to the point where I just didn't know if that was what I wanted to do because the experience I was having was so bad."

Cheri realized that she couldn't keep running away from her old job if she didn't know where she was running to. Instead, she had to do the much more difficult work of figuring out what she really wanted and how that fit into the puzzle of her life and career. Previously Cheri had been a business analyst. She made the mistake of thinking that was enough clarification about what she wanted. After all, she had been in multiple business analyst roles and loved them—a conventional conclusion, but in her situation, the wrong conclusion.

When we met Cheri at HTYC and began working with her on her career change, the first thing that helped her the most was defining what was most important to her in life and career. She was surprised by what she learned: "I wanted to advocate for people whether that meant . . . being the person who was going to stick up for my customers or whether it meant something else. I wanted to be an advocate . . . but I never had put that together before. I also wanted to be a product owner . . . I really like that idea of being a subject-matter expert and owning a process or product. I hadn't been looking for that when I was looking for jobs because I didn't feel like I was qualified for it."

As it turned out, Cheri did continue as a business analyst, but she also become an advocate and a product owner. She did this by becoming completely clear about what she wanted. She ignored almost all of the analyst opportunities available and focused instead on the few that aligned with her ideals.

This is harder than it sounds. Case in point: Cheri's career change took about a year. Although that may seem like a long time, not only was Cheri's career-change process an intentional one, but the role she eventually accepted was significantly different from her previous position. Today she is happy she took the time to define her destination and rework her typical job search method to try something unconventional.

When I spoke to Cheri last, she told me, "The first two weeks I cried every day, but not out of sadness, but because I was laughing. The team is so fantastic and I'm loving what I'm doing... So far, it's just wonderful." Don't you love a happy ending? But wait, this one gets even better: I talked to Cheri as I was writing this, and she told me she had received a promotion to do even more of the work she enjoyed! That's what can happen if you are extraordinarily aligned with your work.

What does it take to make this type of unicorn-level change? It turns out that you need the same type of plan that aerospace engineers use when they design and build commercial jets.

Happen To Checklist

Answer these questions:

- [ ] What are you currently focused on that you're running away from? Think of these as your "don't wants."

- [ ] How could you shift your focus to identifying where you want to "run to"? These are your "wants."

- [ ] Where have you been less intentional in your career in the past? How could you be more intentional going forward?

5

Plan for Inevitable Success

> With the right set of mind, with the right
> people, with the right support, things happen.
>
> GRIGOR DIMITROV

MEET LINNEA. She didn't jump two levels up the promotion ladder. Nope, she jumped four: from senior manager to senior VP. If I were skeptical (I usually am), I would have said, Well, did she go from a big organization to a smaller organization? This is usually how people jump levels easily. But Linnea went to a much larger company, one you've definitely heard of.

Linnea is a self-described multipotentialite (a term coined by my friend Emilie Wapnick in her TEDx talk that's garnered millions of views).1 It means Linnea has a lot of different skills and interests and sometimes has difficulty deciding which one to pursue. After spending thirteen years in the financial services industry, and carrying a newly minted MBA, she came to HTYC so she could determine what to do next. At the time, Linnea's job title was senior strategy consultant. Less than a year later, she had a new job in a new career with the title of senior vice president. Linnea attributes her successful career change to two things: full immersion and extreme preparation. Here's how she described immersing herself in career change:

> One of the things that I did, along with listening to the HTYC podcast, was that I would listen to books as I was driving to work or at the gym. I bought books about specific topics that I was interested in, such as *Wait, How Do I Write This Email?* by Danny Rubin. Same thing with the subject of negotiation. That wasn't my strongest point. So, after listening to Josh Doody's podcast, I bought his book *Fearless Salary Negotiation*, read it, and did the exercises.

And when it came to preparing for meetings and interviews, Linnea did her homework:

> I would say one of the keys to my success was very in-depth preparation for every single interaction that I had, whether it was an informal coffee, whether it was an interview, whether it was following up in an email or a handwritten letter. Every interaction that I had or knew I was going to have, I prepared for to the nth degree. And so that way there was no question that I couldn't answer or anything that I couldn't be prepared for because I genuinely prepared a lot, probably more than I ever have.

What I love about Linnea's story, aside from the great outcome, is that she didn't need any trick or special skill. She understood her purpose, set up her environment, and made time and space in her life for career change so she could work hard on high-impact activities. Linnea is not superhuman. She's simply figured out how to use her gifts, talents, and time differently to get extreme results. You can, too!

Arrival is Not a Matter of Chance

Although every career, and every career change, is different, successful career changers overcome challenges by formulating a plan that makes their career-change success inevitable. I call this plan—wait for it—the plan for inevitable success.

The FAA does not tolerate an airplane flying around that doesn't have systems to ensure it arrives at its destination every single time, because there's simply too much at stake. So, why would you tolerate a plan for career change that also takes your life and work out of your hands?

Granted, when your goal is to become a Happy High Achiever, your situation is different in many ways than boarding an airplane. The main difference is that when you're a human (even a high-performing one) en route to a career change, many more things will likely go wrong than on the average flight.

I don't know about you, but I want a plan for inevitable success. I want to expect the same level of success that air officials, pilots, and passengers all expect when they board an airplane. Even when something fails on the plane, they will still arrive safely at the destination. That's exactly what we aim for at HTYC as we work with clients from all over the world and help them plan for inevitable success.

But here is what you need to know: as you pursue career change, it's not unusual to have to cope with some flight delays and cancellations (since we're speaking about planes). You might be well into making your career change, making great progress, and then your right hand at work accepts another job, leaving you to bear the burden of an increased workload. Or maybe you're reaching out to potential organizations that you'd love to work with and you're getting terrific responses, but all of a sudden it seems like nobody will return your calls, emails, and messages. My wife and I unexpectedly had to find new childcare in the midst of making a career change. If you have children, you know just how much hair can be torn out trying to make sure that your mini humans are cared for.

Sometimes things don't even have to go wrong. What if your current organization says, "Hey guess what, we'd love to give you a promotion." Great, right? Except that you know that all the time and flexibility that you have currently to figure out what you want to be doing will go up in smoke as you ride the learning curve of this new "wonderful" promotion.

The point is, life happens, and it's not going to stop happening because you've decided to make a career change. So let's plan for life to keep happening along the way. Remember that I wrote earlier about how your life and career are interdependent? If you've committed to making a career change, taking hold of the reins and continuing to hold on to what you've declared to be important to you, despite everything else, must be part of the plan. If you're going to do something that few people do, then you'll require a different level of preparation than what you're used to. Olympic runners don't jump from their middle school track-and-field team to earning a berth at the Olympics without massive amounts of intense preparation. Although career change is not the Olympics, it does still require preparation to make it happen. The first part of this plan is psychological: figuring out your purpose.

Figure Out Your Purpose

Let me ask you a question. Why is career change important to you?

Over the past decade my team and I have been asking people this question in conversations, in email, and on forms. We've asked it thousands of times in a multitude of ways, and the answers range widely. Here are some examples:

* "I am feeling unhappy in my current position."
* "Excitement, resume fodder, more money."
* "More opportunities and growth."

What do you notice about these responses? First and foremost, they focus on the respondent's needs. More significantly, each response is missing the deeper purpose—why each person *wants* to change. Purpose is powerful. So powerful that a Harvard study proved those who feel they have a life purpose remain healthier in their later years compared to those who don't feel they have purpose.[2] The example answers above are a start to the question, but they are not purposeful enough to carry people through a challenging career-change process. You need more meaningful reasons to sustain yourself when challenge comes calling.

In her book *Grit: The Power of Passion and Perseverance*, Angela Duckworth defines purpose as "the intention to contribute to the well-being of others."[3] She also talks about what causes people to push through difficulties to success. What she calls grit is often the factor that determines whether a person will ultimately be successful in difficult circumstances. Duckworth also acknowledges that those people who are focused on their purpose are more likely to have grit.

Why? Because reasons that are meaningful to you are more powerful. This means that if you're more emotionally and viscerally connected to your purpose for changing, you have a higher likelihood of making it happen when it gets hard. You can't fake purpose. It's either real or it's not. And if it is real, it can be extraordinarily powerful.

This is why vision boards have grown steadily in popularity since 2010 and the age of Pinterest. However, vision boards used alone don't work, because they're only part of the equation.[4] Purpose is not just about envisioning the result; it's about creating continual action when most people would give up. If you're strategic about your purpose, it can be a powerful moti-vator or even a potent tactic.

When you are identifying purpose, it's important to dig down past the surface level of your answers to the question of why career change is important to you. You can do this by asking yourself, "Why do I want that?" The more your answer strikes an emotional chord with you, the better. Here are a couple exam-ples from HTYC clients:

GOOD	BETTER	BEST
I want to feel good when I go into work each day.	I want to feel appreciated by the people I work with, and I want to feel like the work I'm doing is contributing.	I want to work with people who appreciate that I'm focused on the future but also pay attention to the details. I want to get thank-yous from the people directly affected by my work.
I want flexibility.	I want to be able to make it to my kids' events.	I want my kids to know that they are the most important thing to me and that I will always be there for the important things in their lives.

After identifying the most important reasons for change, many of our clients choose to put this information where they can see it all the time. Sometimes they simply print and post it in a place they will see it daily, like the fridge. Others write on colorful sticky notes and add them to their bathroom mirror or put a notecard in their wallet.

One of the more functional ways you can do this is to create associative reminders. These can be time-based, activity-based, or even visual reminders of why you're doing something. For example, I used to put little ceramic turtles and dinosaurs that my kids had made me in my home office. When I was finding it hard to push through a change and wanted to stop, one glance at a dinosaur would remind me of the reason I wanted to keep going: my children. Another example is adding reminders to your calendar that pop up at key times when you're less likely to be motivated. When I was building HTYC, I went so far as to schedule emails that got sent to my future self about why I was doing this so that I wouldn't give up. When it gets hard, it's important to remember what's at stake.

No matter what your purpose, it must remind you of why you are doing this work to change and that it is the driving force for making the change. The next part of planning for inevitable success is to make sure you've set up your environment to support you.

Set Up Your Environment

I've mentioned the painting company I started that put me through college and even paid for my wife's engagement ring. Most of my employees were students who wanted to earn money over the summer. I had some really amazing employees, but many of the college-aged ones were primarily focused on where their friends were going to be later that day and what bar they would go to that evening. Painting productivity and optimization were the furthest things from their minds. This meant if I wanted them to move fast, I had to make it ridiculously easy for them to focus on the work. My theory was that if all my crew members had systems to rely on, so they didn't waste time finding tools or the location of the jobsite or figuring out which was the concrete paint and which was the siding paint, then the jobs would happen faster and run more smoothly. This meant spending effort at the beginning to get the environment right, which would allow the work to just happen.

First, I went on a near-obsessive hunt to find the perfect boxes to house all the tools my employees might need on the job. Then, I organized those tools so that they could be found with next to no effort. Later on, this same system made it easy for employees to clean up and put everything back into the right place. When my perfect toolbox system began to max out the time saved, I changed my focus to scheduling. What was the best start time? Were eight hours better than ten-hour days? Would lunches or breaks at certain times cause the job to be finished faster or slower?

Although today I know that productivity and effectiveness are about much more than systems and schedules, my original premise is still solid: if you spend a small amount of up-front effort to create an environment that allows you do the work, it keeps you focused on the work later on. This is just as true for painters and job sites as it is for career changers who want to become Happy High Achievers.

Creating a positive environment for change right at the beginning is absolutely worth your effort. What I mean by environment in the case of career change includes things like creating time and space in your schedule, getting others on board with your need for change, and immersing yourself in the process so you can learn. For some people, setting up the environment is the difference between possible and impossible. So think about what you absolutely need to set yourself up for success. Here are some initial questions as a kick-starter:

- What time will you need and what will your schedule look like?

- Where in your schedule do you need to make space to work on this change?

* Whom do you need on your team?

* What forms of accountability do you need?

Make Time and Space

In Chapter 3, I wrote about how one of the biggest obstacles to becoming a Happy High Achiever is a lack of time and energy. But I also wrote about how taking action can be more important than time itself. All that said, when you want to change your career, you must still clear time and space—which involves generating focus and energy (and maybe even literal space)—for the change to take place.

Making time is obvious. What's not obvious is what it takes to do this. It's certainly not taught at schools. It's definitely not taught at most workplaces, and even the blogs out there usually just tell you to "say no more often." Great. Thanks for no help at all.

Remember Linnea, whose story opened this chapter? Linnea took the approach of "full immersion" to make time and space for her career change. Full-immersion career change is the same idea as fully immersing yourself in a culture or country when you're learning a new language. Instead of using language learning apps for fifteen minutes a day and taking years to get to conversational levels, you might go live for three months in a country that speaks the language you want to learn.

To see how to do this, take a look at the schedule that follows. What do you notice? All the normal parts of the day are marked out, but time is also devoted to learning and career change.

Not everyone is going to go full immersion like Linnea. But developing a "master schedule" or a budget for allocating your time over a normal week during your career change is a great way to start making time. Simply going through the act of assigning a job to every hour of the day causes you to assess your time differently.

Time	Schedule	Notes
6:00 AM		
7:00 AM	**6:30–7:35 AM** **Wake up/get ready for day**	Research how to write reach-out email
	7:30 AM **Breakfast**	
8:00 AM	**8:00–8:50 AM** **Commute to work**	Listen to HTYC Podcast
9:00 AM	**9:00 AM** **Check email**	
10:00 AM	**10:00–10:50 AM** **Meeting with boss**	
11:00 AM		
12:00 PM	**12:00–12:50 PM** **Lunch**	Call person with role I'm interested in
1:00 PM	**1:00–1:50 PM** **Meeting with sales team**	
2:00 PM		
3:00 PM		
4:00 PM	4:15 PM **Project wrap-up**	
5:00 PM	**5:00–5:50 PM** **Commute home**	Call former coworker at new company
6:00 PM		
7:00 PM		
8:00 PM	**8:00 PM** **Put kids to bed**	Adjust resume to send to former coworker

Our client Samit put it this way:

Getting really clear on when in the day I will focus on the career change work at the start (and agreeing on that with my partner) has helped me to be able to stick with it. The other important thing has been to have a couple of hours or so every day(!) rather than big chunks of time fewer times in the week, because that helps to fold it all into a routine rather than giving me a potential "excuse" to push the work to another day. In terms of timing, I choose evenings after dinner because that's protected time when I know I'll rarely have something else crop up. My child is asleep and I don't have evening work or calls.

On the following page is an example of what a master schedule might look like in any given week.

Yes, this looks like a simple calendar. But remember this exercise is about starting blank and being forced to intentionally decide what your average week needs to look like so you can successfully make space to focus on career change. This is different from your calendar. It's about giving every hour a category so that you define how you ideally want to spend your time during the week and, more importantly, where you're going to make space in your schedule for career change.

HTYC client Jessica said this about going through this exercise: "I can't even remember how many days I've thought 'No career change stuff today. I'm too busy, I don't have time.' And then the voice in my head says, '*False*, ma'am! You've got time here, here, and here.' #Busted! It really helps keep me accountable for putting in the time."

	MONDAY	TUESDAY	WEDNESDAY
6:00 AM			
7:00 AM			
8:00 AM			
9:00 AM			
10:00 AM	Work		
11:00 AM			
12:00 PM	Lunch & calls/messages for career change		Staff meeting for work
1:00 PM			
2:00 PM	Work		
3:00 PM			Pick up kids
4:00 PM			

Start with blank schedule. Intentionally budget every hour.

THURSDAY	FRIDAY	SATURDAY	SUNDAY

Wake up, coffee & career change work

Shower, get ready for work

Work

Add in time for your career change each week.

Interviews or lunch meetings for career change

Family time

Work

Pick up kids

The TECH Approach to Finding Time and Space

Making the time to focus on career change is not just about finding the time, it's also about becoming aware about what expectations surround *how* you spend your time.

Now, you might be saying, "Uh, Scott, you don't know what you're talking about! I really only have two hours available after work to get one kid to sports, get the other kid to do homework, get the first kid back from sports, then feed them and get them into bed. If you're talking about expectations, and my kids expect to eat, are you telling me not to feed my kids?"

No, I'm definitely not telling you to withhold food from your kids so that you can make a career change, although I have teenagers and it would definitely have a positive impact on the grocery expenses! There's almost always more here once we start digging deeper into what expectations have an impact on your time. We do this using what I call the TECH approach.

TIME
Identify what is pulling on your time.

EXPECTATION
Pinpoint where the expectation is coming from.

CONVERSATION
Determine what courageous conversation needs to take place to change it.

HAPPEN
Happen to it—have the conversation.

Suspend your judgment and read on as I show you how the TECH approach works using an example from one of our clients, whom we'll call Carla. First, we looked at how Carla was spending her time (T) and identified what the expectations (E) were around it.

Time	Activity	Expectation
6:00 AM	**WORKOUT** →	*expectation of self*
8:00 AM	**DROP OFF KIDS** →	*partner, self*
8:30 AM	**WORK** →	*boss, coworkers, customers*
3:00 PM	**PICK UP KIDS** →	*partner, teachers, judgy parents (and kids)*
5:15 PM	**LATE MEETING** →	*self, boss*
6:30 PM	**MAKE DINNER** →	*self, family expectations*
8:30 PM	**GET KIDS IN BED** →	*expect to be tired*

When Carla looked at what was taking her time, she said what people always say at first: "I don't think I can really change any of this. I mean, I guess I could not work out, but I feel terrible when I don't."

That's when we started asking questions to identify what kind of conversations she needed to have (C):

- What would it take to have someone else drop the kids off at school?

- Do you need to start work at 8:30 am every day?

- Could your partner make dinner a few days a week for just a few months?

- What is keeping you at work late each day?

- Could you persuade the project manager who gives you a long weekly update (that is useless and that you hate being there for) to send you an email update instead, unless actual input or discussion is needed?

As we started poking and prodding at Carla's schedule, it became apparent that some of the expectations and demands on her time were necessary (hard expectations) and some were unnecessary (soft expectations).

Next, Carla had the courageous conversations (H) she needed to. Her family needed dinner, but once she had a conversation with her partner, he was totally willing to support her by making dinner a couple nights a week. She needed to be at work, but it was unnecessary for her to start before 10 am some days. Once she had the conversation, she was surprised to discover that her boss and coworkers were fully supportive of her starting work at 10 am on Fridays each week.

Of course, your schedule will be different than Carla's. However, we see the same pattern over and over at HTYC. At first many people believe they don't have the time or space. Once they dig into the expectations around their time, they find that change is possible.

SINCE I'VE been discussing expectations around time, let me finish off this chapter on planning for inevitable success by addressing what your expectations might be about how long career change takes.

At HTYC we've seen our clients take anywhere from three months to eighteen months to find their next career, with the average journey taking about eight months in length. I point this out not because you need to get locked into the thought of this being a year-long transition. It might not be, but the point is you should prepare yourself as though it will take that long, because not doing so won't set you up for inevitable success.

Instead, I encourage you to think critically about what areas you need to work on to build your own plan for inevitable success. If you're struggling with finding your purpose or making time, a mentor or professional can help you create your plan. The quest for career change is never the same for any two people, which is why it's hard. But if you want to become a Happy High Achiever, this level of preparation and consideration—a plan for inevitable success—is a prerequisite.

Once you've built your plan, the next step is clarity. At least that's what everyone thinks. In the next chapter we will discuss how to drink wine for a living and what an executive formerly in charge of Disney World can teach us about priorities.

Happen To Checklist

Answer these questions:

- [ ] Where do you believe you will struggle the most in your career-change process? What can you do to proactively plan for that?

- [ ] Where are the expectations coming from that compete for your time? What courageous conversations do you need to have to temporarily make time and space for your change?

Happen To Bonus

Visit happentoyourcareer.com/bonus to see an example of a completed plan for inevitable success and get a template to create your own.

6

Declare Your Priorities

Nobody's life is ever all balanced. It's a conscious decision to choose your priorities every day.

ELISABETH HASSELBECK

I F YOU look at Kristy Wenz's Instagram, you'll think she's on vacation all the time. Actually, she's doing the work she loves as a contractor for numerous organizations for which she created the roles that fit her career goals and personal values. She wears a lot of hats and handles many responsibilities, including traveling to vineyards and tasting wine.

How did she pull that off? She knew what she wanted.

After twenty years in marketing and PR, Kristy wanted the usual trappings of fulfilling work, but she was also looking for a few other things in her new career, as she explained: "I knew I wanted to write. I knew I wanted to somehow be involved in food and wine and travel because I love how it brings people together." Kristy also wanted her career to connect her to history and culture.

Travel? Wine? History and culture? Those aren't career goals, those are stops on a European vacation, right? Wrong. Not only did Kristy create a role for herself that checked all her unique career-goal boxes, but she also established a situation that met every item on her list. Here's how Kristy describes her work:

> I needed something that was going to be flexible and allow me to work remotely. I put in a lot of time, but on my schedule, which is wonderful, especially as a mom. I get to write, I get to be a manager, I get to jump in with ideas, I have a seat at the table and work with a dynamic group of people who are really amazing, and that was important to me, as well. Just working with like-minded people. People with similar values and the same goals and missions that I have. Everything fell into line, and I honestly did not think it was possible even six months ago.

Kristy had the audacity to ask for what she wanted. Then she went out and got it. How? Well, the first thing Kristy did was take a hiatus from work. She and her family moved to Europe for several months. Kristy hoped the time away would give her clarity about her next step. It didn't work.

This is a mistake that many people make when they are searching for clarity in their work or other areas of their life. We believe that if we can give ourselves the time or space, we will find the elusive clarity that we're looking for. Although time, space, and energy are all helpful for getting perspective, they by no means guarantee clarity. That's not at all how clarity works.

If you search your favorite book-buying website, you will find hundreds of books on the topic of clarity. Clarity for teachers, clarity and calm, the clarity journal, a year of clarity, ten years of clarity, thirty days to clarity, and my personal favorite, *The Pool Maintenance Logbook: Your Personal Guide to Water Clarity* (we just got a hot tub, so this is important).

Let me ask you some questions: Why do you want clarity in the first place? And why do you think having clarity is a solution? And what is clarity even? Before you buy *Clarity for Teachers*, volume 7, shouldn't you know what this clarity is that we're all after?

Whether you need clarity for retaining calm, finding your path, or preventing awkward moments with the neighbors when you fling open the hot tub cover to find green swamp water, we all seem to want clarity. And even if we don't want it, we still think we should find it. I've found that when I ask people about what clarity is or why they want it, they say things like

* "If I only knew what it was that I wanted to be doing, I could then go and do it."

* "I want clarity so I can finally know what it is that I want to be when I grow up. I've just never found it."

We act as though clarity is like a certification or degree: that once we have it, we'll finally be able to progress to the next level. But clarity is not a level to achieve that then allows us to move on. Clarity is actually a *result*.

What do I mean? Well, if you take the time to look up the etymology of the word clarity, you'll notice "clarity" and "declare" have the same root: *clarare*. In Latin, *de clarare* means "to thoroughly make clear." This means that you get clarity from the act of declaring. Notice it doesn't translate to "find clear," "arrive at clear," or "randomly happen to have clear smack you upside the head."

The verb "make" is active. It's something you can do, an action you can take. Clarity comes from declaring what's most important to you and actively making clear. This active means to clarity comes from you deciding and proclaiming that some things are most important to you, not from waiting for that thing to show up in your life.

That means getting clarity is a prioritization problem, *not* a knowledge problem.

Think about that for a second. You can have clarity at any point in time. This is empowering. This thing that everyone is looking for is right on your doorstep waiting for you to answer

HOW PEOPLE THINK CLARITY WORKS

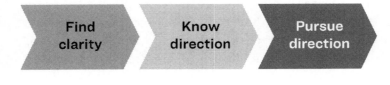

HOW CLARITY ACTUALLY WORKS

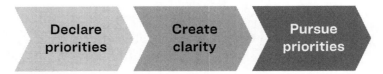

the door. But it's also not as simple as just declaring that spending time with your partner or your family is the most important thing and being done with it. Or saying, "I want to spend my time doing meaningful work," and then *poof*, you are good to go! That doesn't help either. Declaring something as most important to you requires two active ingredients: courage and prioritization.

I remember having a conversation with Lee Cockerell, the former executive VP of Walt Disney World; he is the reason Disney Paris exists. I asked him how he made sure he is living his most important priorities, and he shared this story with me: "My wife called my office one day when I was first starting out. I told her I was in a meeting. When I got home at night, she said, 'Lee, who's more important than me?' I said, 'Nobody.' She said, 'So why don't you take my call?' From that day on, I told my secretary, 'When my wife calls, always put her through if she wants to talk to me.'"

His solution was simple: make the most important things the most important.

When Lee told me this story, I felt like this insight was revolutionary. But it's not revolutionary at all. It is, however, vastly different from the way most of us operate. This is because it requires the foresight to declare priorities and also the courage to act upon them in a world where acting on your priorities is often socially unacceptable.

The great news is that it's far easier to find courage when you know what your priorities are. Then, what makes it easier to know what your priorities are? I'm going to share a simple tool for identifying and declaring your priorities. At HTYC we call this tool the Ideal Career Profile, and this is exactly what I will discuss in the next part of this book.

Happen To Checklist

Answer these questions:

☐ What are the highest priorities in your life?

☐ Does your work accommodate those priorities? If not, which ones need to be accommodated?

PART THREE

THE SEVEN ELEMENTS OF MEANINGFUL WORK

7

Sometimes We Only *Think* We Know What We Want

When your values are clear to you,
making decisions becomes easier.

ATTRIBUTED TO ROY E. DISNEY

WHEN I met Eric, he was working as an engineer for a gas company in Las Vegas, Nevada. Everything was fine. Except that Eric felt that by working there, he was helping to systematically destroy the planet. Okay, maybe not that harsh, but Eric cared about the environment and he cared about doing good for future generations. He cared about having a positive impact on the world, and working as an engineer for the gas company felt like the antithesis of everything he stood for. Combine that with continuous nine-to-fourteen-hour workdays, and the job had him questioning nearly everything in his life.

However, when Eric came to work with us, he appeared clear about what he wanted to do. He wanted to work for a solar energy company and even had a few in mind. His reasoning was that a company that produces renewable energy was a cause he could stand behind. It aligned with his morals and values. But it turned out that working in the solar industry was the furthest thing from what he actually wanted, even though it all seemed so right at first glance. Why was he so far off the mark?

Eric wasn't unique in this situation. I've seen this phenomenon countless times. We think we understand what it is we want and need, only to later find out that what we imagined we wanted was partially or entirely wrong.

To understand, let's go to one of my favorite psychology books, *Stumbling on Happiness* by Harvard professor Daniel Gilbert. Gilbert has made an entire career of using science to uncover the illusions we have about ourselves. In this book, Gilbert points out that we are usually wrong when we imagine what would make us happy in the future. This is because the imagination, while useful for creative projects and dreaming big, has multiple shortcomings when predicting the future about how we will feel *after* those dreams come true.

Gilbert makes his point through a series of studies in which test subjects predicted how they would feel after an event, like winning a gift card for an ice cream parlor and then completing a boring task, or losing out on free pizza after eating potato chips. The study divided the test subjects into two groups: those who had an opportunity to talk to people who had experienced the event previously, and those who had no exposure to people who had experienced the event. Both groups were asked to indicate how they would feel after the event. The test subjects who had the benefit of talking to people with experience of the event were consistently more accurate in indicating how they might feel than the group who were asked to imagine how they would feel.

This premise extends far beyond your feelings about junk food. Our imaginations are consistently poor predictors of how we will feel in the future about many events, from job loss all the way to—you guessed it—career choice. This means we need to consult what has been proved by research to make us happy, rather than rely on our imagination alone.

Fortunately, there is a great body of available information on happiness, especially as it relates to work. When we use research on what's already been proved for humans combined with specific knowledge about ourselves, we can understand what creates fulfilling work. For a complete list of my favorite books and studies on happiness, make sure to review the resources at the back of this book.

But sometimes the research can be overwhelming, precisely because there are so many areas to consider when thinking about what makes fulfilling work for you. To help you cut through all the chatter, we use the Ideal Career Profile (ICP).

To be clear, even with this tool and the current research available, it still isn't easy to define what will work for you. When we're working with clients, it usually takes two to four months to create an accurate first version of an ICP, and it can take longer when you don't have access to help and expertise.

The ICP is a full picture of the who, what, when, where, and how you are targeting in your ideal career. It is an in-depth profile that helps you understand what you need from your work and what factors are critical for you. Think about the ICP as a big checklist of all the criteria you need for fulfilling work.

Before you're ready to create your own profile of fulfilling work, you must first understand the elements that contribute to a fulfilling career. Many things have an impact on fulfilling work, but there are seven key elements that have a significantly higher impact than all others:

1 **Contribution:** how well your work supports your desire to help others and make an impact

2 **Flexibility and autonomy:** how much freedom you have in how you work

3 **Quality of life:** how well your work supports other areas of your life

4 **Growth:** how much your work offers the potential for learning, creativity, variety, and feedback

5 **Signature strengths:** how well your work takes advantage of your talents, predispositions, and abilities

6 **Supportive people:** how much you feel supported by your colleagues and your boss

7 **Values:** how much your work allows you to be who you are, or want to become, and matches what you value most

Unfortunately, most of us don't realize that we have these needs; they become apparent only when they are missing. When you're missing any one of these areas for a significant length of time, your work will feel less fulfilling. Conversely, if you have all of these areas consistently, your work feels much more fulfilling.

We tend to search for one "best" way to solve our problems. When I spoke with Gretchen Rubin, the bestselling author of *The Happiness Project* and *The Four Tendencies,* we discussed some of the drawbacks to how our "research" around problem-solving occurs. The challenge is, of course, that identifying fulfilling work is a complex problem, meaning that it is a problem that is dependent on other problems. When you have complex problems, whether it's climate change or identifying what creates fulfilling work for you, it's difficult to untangle the main problem from all the individual problems, let alone identify a solution to any one of them.

In their book *Decisive,* brothers Chip and Dan Heath point out that humans have a tendency toward what they call "narrow framing." This is when we look for a solution to a problem with a narrow focus, often reducing decisions to, "Should I do this or not?" They also point out that confirmation bias can cause us to look favorably upon the evidence that reinforces our initial beliefs about a potential solution to a problem. This can lead us to become overly focused on the "one solution" to rule them all.

Since we know now that fulfilling work is a complex problem, it makes sense that one simple solution is almost never the answer.

For example, Eric, our oil and gas engineer, thought that a job in the solar industry was the answer for him. He eventually found that he was looking for impact and meaning, but the ways he needed it most were much more subtle than simply an industry change. He ended up making a change to a highly supportive small organization that had a family feel to it, while still getting to use his engineering skills and work closely with his team to make an impact. This unique combination of relationships, type of work, and type of support, where he could see his contribution, was much closer to his ideal.

We tend to believe that one thing is the answer. It's not. The answer involves identifying what's most important, then staying in the zone of those areas and finding the right combination for you.

You might look at this and say, "Okay, that's not too hard." The challenge is that the particular combination of the seven elements of an ideal career is unique for everyone. For example, what constitutes fulfilling work for me, such as work that helps others (contribution), might be different for you. Finding the right fit usually isn't about finding the right occupation but about identifying the right combination of these seven elements for you. Once you know that, only then can you allow the work into your life that reliably matches up with that combination.

The Context Matters

When you are exploring what defines meaningful work for you, it's important to notice that subtle context differences can be the difference between hugely fulfilling or horrifically meaningless work. Each person needs to identify the contexts that are important for them. "Important" means that the right context makes a significant difference in your quality of life and work, and when that context is missing, it can take an otherwise great situation and make it feel unfulfilling at best and downright pointless at worst.

I like to think about context in terms of four areas: people, problems, tasks, and scope. When you think about meaningful work, some of these areas may be well aligned with your needs, but others may not. This can create confusion about whether an opportunity is purposeful or creating meaning for you.

For example, if you're a marketing director in a healthy-meal delivery subscription company, you might feel that your job of reaching hundreds of thousands of people (scope) through content marketing (task) is a way to help people. This might become even more meaningful for you if helping people eat healthily (problem) was important to you because you had serious health problems in the past that you overcame by changing your eating habits. This emotional connection to the problem makes it even more meaningful. Maybe your company is targeting at-risk people who are the age at which you made your shift, so you can identify specifically with these people you're impacting.

Now, let's look at that context in reverse. Let's say you're still in that marketing director role in the same meal delivery subscription company, but this time your context needs are different. Maybe it feels most rewarding to you when you have one-to-one interactions with people (scope). This single misalignment could make your day-to-day job of reaching hundreds of thousands of people feel meaningless overall because you don't get to interact directly with the people who are benefiting from the healthy meals and see the results.

As I cover each of the seven elements of fulfilling work, pay attention to the context that makes sense for you. I'll also offer up some examples of what it looks like when that element is already present in your work, or what it might look like when you're missing it. After I discuss the elements, I will show you how to pull all seven together to create your own unique profile of your ideal career.

Let's start by looking at the one element of meaningful work that almost all of us are pulled toward but tend to think we are unique in pursuing: the desire to help others.

Happen To Checklist

Answer these questions:

☐ What do you feel is missing from your work right now?

☐ What is already great about your work (or past work) that you want to keep?

Happen To Bonus

Go to happentoyourcareer.com/quiz and take an assessment that will help you understand which of the seven elements of fulfilling work you're missing and identify what you need.

8

Contribution

Passion is the wrong word. I think professionals care about challenge and contribution. Passion is about you. Contribution is about other people.

DAN PINK

MY TEAM at HTYC often has conversations with people from all over the world who want to find or create more fulfilling work. It's one of the most fun parts of our jobs. Cindy often tells me, "I got to make eight new friends today." Cindy has had many of these conversations and loves them all (except for the one person who showed up drunk and asked her how to lie on her resume—you know who you are). She also knows that somewhere in the conversation she'll hear a declaration she's heard many times: "I've realized that I want to help people."

We never get bored of hearing this declaration, but couldn't we argue that every job in the world is helping people in some way or another? Whether you deliver food or help people detox, whether you're a pastor or a project manager, an executive or an event coordinator, aren't you helping people? So why do so many people feel like they're not?

The secret to feeling more fulfilled is directly seeing and connecting with how you're helping people. If you were literally changing the lives of a billion people on the planet but couldn't see how what you were doing affected them, you might not feel like you were helping people.

Google is a great example of this. They have a product that has an impact on many people. Their search engine and ads reach people nearly everywhere on earth; their productivity apps change the way many people work (I use Google Docs to collaborate in real time with my team and even wrote this book on it). Google is consistently on nearly every list that includes "best" and "place to work" in the title. Yet, I still hear from Google employees who come to us that their work feels empty. As one person I spoke with put it, "At some point getting more clicks just feels meaningless."

It's not about the work itself; it's that *you* directly see and connect with *how* the work is helping people. Or you don't. Does this mean that if you get too far removed, you will never see how you're helping others? Should you always be working one-on-one with people? Not necessarily.

When I was in HR leadership for a Fortune 500 food company, we had a facility that produced a well-known brand of microwave meals. In that facility, there were operators working on different pieces of machinery. If you asked them what they did, many of the operators would simply tell you that they made TV dinners. But the operator of the gravy machine in the facility had a different story. When you asked him what he did, he would tell you he was feeding families. To my knowledge he rarely interacted directly with the customers who ate the gravy he made, but he still found purpose and meaning in his work because he could directly see and connect with how it was helping others.

What all of this means is that you have to define your own version of how you want to help others. The scope of helping others can vary widely. You can help in different ways at different levels. This can be helping individuals, or you can help groups, communities, cities, states, or even nations. Some people need a one-on-one impact to feel like they are helping. Others need to make an impact on large groups. Here are some quotes from HTYC surveys that illustrate what it sounds like when you directly see and connect with how you're helping others:

* "I love when people tell me that I've made a difference in their day."

* "I have this desire to provide individual experiences. I get to do that daily."

* "My favorite part is when I get to see the difference I've made in the community."

And this is what it sounds like when you don't:

* "I don't feel like I'm making a difference in the world. I'm in IT and buried in bureaucracy as I try to navigate my projects."

9

Flexibility and Autonomy

Find autonomy in your job... Autonomy is key to feeling good about the work you do, no matter what kind of work it is.

JEAN CHATZKY

I F YOU'RE reading this book, it's a safe bet you fall into one of two categories: you either want more flexibility and autonomy in your work, or you want to maintain the same amount you already have in your next career opportunity.

The reason this is a sure-fire bet is that research proves continuously that how work gets done matters to people all over the world. I've read hundreds of articles, abstracts, and studies, and the common conclusion among all of them is that people deeply want the freedom to decide or influence how their work gets done.

When I say "how the work gets done," what I mean is that you can choose the timing involved in doing your work, whether that is when your deadlines are, when you take time off, or even how long your day might be. But it also includes the autonomy to decide how you will go about doing the work or getting a particular result. When you don't have the ability to influence or decide when or how your work gets done, the results can be severe.

The need to feel some control in your life is thrown drastically out of alignment when flexibility and autonomy are missing from your work. The stress it places on your mind and body is absolutely real. Many studies found higher rates of physical and mental illness when flexibility and autonomy were missing in a work role.[1] Several studies even linked lack of work autonomy with higher instances of heart disease.[2]

Setting the research aside, you have already read about how this can happen in the stories I've shared. Michael, our finance executive in the first chapter, had a good gig with a major movie studio until he was thrown into a situation that perpetually felt out of control. That's when he lost twenty pounds from all the stress. Another HTYC client, Louie, started having seizures when he moved into a role where he felt unable to influence how the work got done. Alissa experienced temporary blindness at her HR role. What's clear in all these stories is that almost everyone (individuals and companies) consistently underrates just how valuable it is to influence or decide how the work gets done.

Over the years, many of my roles have involved me providing development and training sessions. One of the things I learned early on in my training career was to create a curiosity gap that would cause people to want to learn at the beginning of the session. You've seen this technique before if you've ever watched a movie that begins in the middle of the story.

Imagine this scene: The main character, wearing a bright red raincoat, is being pursued on foot through Miami. She parkours over a burning car, climbs a fire escape, and leaps from building to building as an explosion happens in the background and then . . . the movie cuts to ten years before this event. All the questions you have about why the character is on the run go unanswered. Maybe you want to know why she was wearing that raincoat in Miami when it was most definitely not raining. Is she just well-prepared, or is that part of some present-day hero costume? Whatever you're wondering, your curiosity is engaged and you want answers!

What does this have to do with flexibility and autonomy? Well, I often begin training sessions with questions designed to spark multiple responses but for which there is no one answer. I once started a leadership training workshop by asking what micromanagement is. After getting an assortment of answers such as, "It's a mortal sin," and, "Where your manager is all up in your biz-nass," it became apparent that nobody could quite put their finger on what micromanagement is, even though everyone agreed that it is universally detested.

Don't worry, though; I'll tell you. Micromanagement is when—

(Cut to scene of me sitting and putting on my shoes, a red raincoat hanging on the back of the chair).

Just kidding!

Much of what is called micromanagement is the opposite of what you are looking for in "how" you do your work. It's removing all the creativity or dictating everything down to the minute about when you will work, even when that conflicts with some time off that you might need. Micromanagement is when your boss tells you that you need to do something their way without explaining why, even when you find a better way to do it that will save the company money and take less effort. Though mildly annoying at best, often it's downright maddening. Sadly, micromanagement dissolves trust in the workplace, which is a critical component of autonomy.[3]

Some people need more support than others to feel that their work is meaningful, so it's critical you think carefully about what you consider to be micromanagement in the context of how you do your work. Although we can universally agree that we don't want micromanagement, it's more important to identify what we do want. What is the right context for you? What does great support look like for you? The right blend for "how you work" is different from person to person. You might prefer to have complete autonomy and total creativity in your work, or you might prefer to work with a mentor or a team to create specific structure around projects.

Where flexibility is concerned, this also varies between individuals. For example, I have a friend who does his best work in the late afternoon or early evening, but I prefer to start early, and my best hours are from 10 am to about 1:30 pm—I'm pretty much useless from 2 pm to 4 pm. For some people, flexibility might mean that they need to be available for their obligations or desires outside of work. Maybe they need to be available to pick up the kids from school or to take time off to help an elderly family member. For others, flexibility means having the freedom to go to medical appointments or yoga classes, or even to head out with friends.

Flexibility and autonomy over how and when you work is number two in this list for a good reason, because when you feel trapped or hemmed in by your work, it can make you miserable. Even if you are not completely miserable, being unable to meet your commitments and obligations consistently outside work adds stress to your life. And that's how this element of meaningful work overlaps with the next element of fulfilling work: your quality of life. That's why it's absolutely key you explore the dynamics of flexibility and autonomy and think honestly about how work fits into your life in this way.

When flexibility is missing in your work it often sounds like this:

- "I want more flexibility with my time. I also would like to do something that I'm good at *and* that I enjoy. I love helping people, but I hate being stuck at a computer in an office all day."

- "I need more. I no longer am willing to settle. I enjoy learning, I crave nature, and I would love a flexible schedule (or, better yet, to work from home so that I could work anywhere)!"

And here's what flexibility sounds like when you do have it:

- "I love that my team trusts me to do my best work when I want to work. I'm so much better from 4 pm to 7 pm than I am at 9 am, when everyone else on my team begins work. It's great that we can work together during the times that make sense for us instead of having to be there from nine to five every day."

- "I have a special needs child. I often need to be available during the normal work week, and my work environment allows me to be there for my family. I can be fully at work when I'm working. I'm grateful to have this level of trust and flexibility."

10

Quality of Life

> The quality of our relationships
> determines the quality of our lives.
>
> **ESTHER PEREL**

WHEN I met Andrea, she was an overworked project manager in Toronto. She had heard other stories of career changes on our podcast and reached out to us after she thought there could be more to life than sixty-plus-hour work weeks, insane commutes, and rarely seeing her significant other. She shared that her work felt pointless. Why was she spending so much time for so little money if she wasn't getting anything in return?

She's not the only person to come to this conclusion. If your work doesn't support the other priority areas of your life, then it becomes an obstacle to your fulfilment. Worse yet, if you have the six other areas nailed but your work isn't supporting the most important areas of your life outside of work, then eventually it will turn an otherwise amazing situation into a net negative.

This happens most commonly when something outside of your work changes. In Andrea's case she had once felt great about her work. Then her hours crept up, but her pay didn't, and she began wanting to spend more time with people outside work who were important to her. The same thing happened to me when I worked at Target. I loved working for them, and the job hit all the elements of fulfilling work for me. But then I had kids, and the work schedule began to conflict with the time I instead wanted to spend with them.

Kids, significant others, family, and friends aren't the only examples of work supporting the life you want to lead. For example, work must help you meet your financial obligations and goals. If you're not getting paid enough to keep the lights on and pay for indoor plumbing, then your work isn't going to feel fulfilling for long, no matter how good it is in other areas. I've seen this struggle with those who have a career in ministry, teaching, and non-profit organizations. Many people choose to leave an otherwise rewarding situation because they aren't making enough money to support their families or meet their financial goals.

Conversely, it feels fulfilling when you have a situation that supports what is important to you outside of work. I once spoke to a guy who was a highly rated ice hockey referee. He absolutely loved officiating and made great money doing it, but it was only during a portion of the year. Any job that didn't allow him to continue to officiate ice hockey would take him further from where he wanted to be, not closer. His work needed to be able to support the way he wanted to live his life.

This is a vastly different way to think about it, but for your work to be fulfilling, it needs to support the other important areas in your life.

Here's what it sounds like when your work is not supportive of the other areas of your life:

- "I've hardly seen my friends and family at all for almost three months. We're going through a challenging time at work right now with the merger. I just hope it will be over in the next few months."

* "There's a non-profit that I want to be involved with, but my work obligations really don't allow me to."

* "I've been worried about saving for retirement for years, but even when we've cut our spending, we still can barely contribute the bare minimum for employer-matching 401K. I'm worried that it's nowhere near enough, but I'm already at the top of my pay scale."

And this is what it sounds when your work supports the other areas of your life:

* "I love to travel. It's a big part of my life to be able to explore other countries and cultures. Having work that is supportive of me traveling while I'm working is everything to me. I couldn't do with the normal two weeks of vacation."

* "My partner and I have a goal to have $2.5 million net worth by the time we're forty-five. We both plan to continue working after that, but it means we will never be forced to spend time at companies or jobs we don't want to. Fortunately, we're on track because my company pays me well."

11

Growth

If we are growing we are always going
to be outside our comfort zone.

JOHN MAXWELL

WHEN PEOPLE ask me how this company got started, if I'm feeling cheeky, I will tell them I made more career changes before I was thirty years old than their aunt, brother, and next-door neighbor combined. And this is absolutely true. I've had many jobs and occupations, in various companies and industries.

But nobody ever asks me why. Why have I moved around so much from job to job? Other than the fact that I found it was easy to increase my salary through negotiation each time I changed jobs, there was one driving factor: I was bored. Very bored.

When some people get bored, they can force themselves to keep going. That was most definitely not me. Early in my career, when I had become proficient in whatever skill I was learning, or when I had mastered some of the initial challenges, I was pretty much done with a job. I have ADD, and until I learned to manage the challenges of this, my brain would involuntarily tap out when I was feeling bored. Then it would take everything in me to force myself to do my job. If I wasn't careful, this would lead to my work performance dipping and awkward conversations with my boss about how I had gone from rock star to rock bottom. So I learned to compensate by making career changes before rock bottom happened. I now know that these career changes were because my learning had slowed down. The challenges I found super fun were no longer challenging; the variety and novelty of a job became familiar and rare, and my growth rate would dip.

Although you may be far better than me at avoiding awkward conversations with your boss because your performance stays high, it doesn't change the fact that at a fundamental level we all require growth. This need for growth manifests in four ways: variety of work, opportunity for creativity, feedback from your work or team, and on-going challenge. Combined, these create learning, and when that learning is applied to your identity, skills, or behavior, it fuels growth.

When good growth is abundant in your job, it often sounds like this:

- "My role with my company has shifted several times in the last few years. I never get bored. I'm continuously learning."

- "I'm working with an organization that's rapidly growing, so even though I've been in product development the whole time, I always need to learn something new."

- "I get to work in health care technology. It's a subject matter that's really interesting and important to me. I could spend the next ten years diving deeper into this topic."

When your work is missing growth, it can sound like this:

- "It drives me crazy that I've never ever known what I wanted to be when I grow up. I've gone through a couple different types of careers. Originally, I had a 'problem' of becoming good at something, then getting bored and wanting to move on to the next thing. This left me bored and in need of searching."

* "Sitting in front of a screen drawing technical details lacks the variety I need."

* "I am not happy, not challenged, and not living the life I desire."

Like the other elements needed for an ideal career, what creates great growth for one person is different for the next person. Someone who considers themselves to be a rapid learner might need a different rate of growth than someone who is more methodical and needs to master things one step at a time.

If the honeymoon period in a job wears off quickly for you, then you may need to align yourself with an organization that has the right type of growth for you. And if you need more structure within which to grow, then find an organization that supports and values that.

12

Signature Strengths

The good life consists in deriving happiness by
using your signature strengths every day in the
main realms of living. The meaningful life adds
one more component: using these same strengths
to forward knowledge, power or goodness.

MARTIN SELIGMAN

THE MINNESOTA-BASED retail giant Target is famous for
keeping ahead of the trends and causing shoppers to walk
in for avocados and toilet paper and walk out with $200
worth of groceries, clothes, toys, and sporting goods that
they are convinced they need.

Let me tell you that if you're choosing to walk into a Target
store, then you're choosing to gamble against the house with the
odds stacked against you. This is the same company that used
gait recognition technology to identify recurring shoplifters by
how they walked and was able to identify patterns in shopping
to predict when a customer is pregnant. (Imagine how awkward
that is when a coupon for strollers comes to the house but the
significant other isn't quite in the loop yet.)

But Target understands not only consumer behavior but employee behavior as well. This was the first place I had exposure to world-class development, and also the first place where I encountered the term "signature strengths." Years later, I learned that positive psychologist Martin Seligman had coined the term. If you read enough books on happiness, you eventually realize that many of them riff off Seligman's ground-breaking work. Seligman defines signature strengths as "those character strengths that are most essential to who we are."[1] In my observation, the phrase "essential to who we are" is absurdly on point. But what's the big deal with signature strengths anyway?

Gallup is a consulting company that most people have heard of. If you visit their website, they say they help organizations "solve their most pressing problems."[2] Although this is a big claim, Gallup is in a unique position to achieve this mission because they have over 35 million respondents in their database. And the company's research consistently shows that having an opportunity to use strengths regularly matters. Here's just a small sample of the findings:

- You gain a positive emotional boost while using your strengths.

- The more you use your strengths in a day, the less likely you are to feel stressed, worried, angry, or sad.

- When you use your strengths regularly, you are more likely to have positive emotions regularly.

Now pair these findings with Seligman's definition of signature strengths: those things that are essential to who we are. Aren't you most likely to be happiest when you get to be yourself, or when you're at your best?

Hearing about signature strengths during my time at Target changed everything for me. What if I could spend all day working in my strengths? What if I could optimize my entire life for my strengths? How enjoyable would it be? Would I be laughing hysterically and joyful all the time?

Gallup research has us covered there too. They've found that those who report experiencing happiness, enjoyment, smiling, or even laughing a lot use their strengths more than those who don't. Not a surprise, but how much more is it, really? And what's the smallest change that you can make to see different results?

Gallup found that using your strengths as little as one to two hours more per day buys you the ticket to feeling like you're on the career happiness joy ride. From the results we've seen with our clients, it's more like buying a fast pass at Disney World. Conversely, at HTYC we've also seen the opposite: when you stop working in your strengths for even as little as six months, this can have a devastating psychological impact and erode your confidence.

Research, and the experiences of our clients, shows that you get results quickly when you regularly start connecting with and using your signature strengths. If you visit a financial advisor or read a blog post on investing, you eventually get hit over the head with the "magic" of compound interest. If you invest $2,000 a month ($24,000 in a year) and it has a 10 percent return, that produces $2,400 in interest for you. But if you continually invest that same $2,000 a month for twenty years, your investment grows to a grand total of $1,518,737.67! Strengths function the same way. As you start working more and more in your signature strengths, you'll see a compounding effect.

When I met Maggie, who was working in communications at the time, she said she felt stuck. She knew she wanted to be doing something different, but she didn't know what. As she started exploring what she could do next, she began leaning into areas that came more naturally. She ended up creating a presentation for a training program, a project that was fun and relatively easy for her compared to other people. She noted this as a piece of evidence in her exploration, and pretty soon she realized that she was particularly well suited for training and development.

Fast forward several months, and Maggie was working within her existing organization to make a shift into training. This is where it gets interesting. Sixteen months later, I received a message from Maggie. She had been promoted. When I spoke with her just eighteen months after that, Maggie was getting promoted again. Each time, she was getting a title increase and a pay increase. More importantly, she was enjoying the experience.

Here's what was happening. Each time she found ways to use her signature strengths, she got more joy out of work. She was contributing more and becoming that person whom people view as a high performer and want to be around. This led to additional promotions that pushed her deeper into her strengths. By exploring and focusing on her signature strengths, Maggie was led to not just one, but multiple executive-level roles that she's actively enjoyed.

Strengths make you who you are. They are key to your success, but sometimes your signature strengths (or your version of the "Force") may appear to have a shadow or a dark side to them.

Take, for example, one of our HTYC clients, Sachin. I met Sachin when he was a senior consultant with a well-known consulting company. As we worked together, the things he wasn't good at doing kept surfacing as hurdles in his Ideal Career Profile. But then he had a realization that turned this thinking on its head.

Ever since Sachin was a little kid, his friends and parents had labeled him as obsessive. He would organize everything, everywhere. He couldn't help it, even though it became an ongoing joke. "Oh, that's just Sachin," they would say.

In one conversation, Sachin confided in me that he couldn't even sit down to get some work done in a hotel room until he put the lamp back "in place" and straightened the picture. Up until then, he had looked at this need to organize as a negative, his dark side, and he felt powerless to change, which had the effect of making him feel ashamed. But that same need to organize was embedded deeply under the surface of everything that was good in his life, too. This intense need for organization was Sachin's signature strength and essential to who he was. As a consulting team leader, it was the reason he was so successful in creating plans that were executed and why many people wanted to be on the same projects as him. When Sachin was involved in the project, things just went well, seemingly miraculously.

Sachin realized that he was viewing his signature strength from the dark side. When he saw that his overwhelming need to organize was what caused him to be successful in the first place, he changed. All of a sudden, identifying where he should be spending his time and what would create a great career for him became much more obvious. More importantly, he realized that he did not need a massive career change but to lean into the areas of his current situation that allowed him to put his obsessive organizational ability to good use.

This can be true for you, too. If a career change to work that fits you is to be possible, you will need to understand what signature strengths you bring to the table. Once you are fully aware of how your signature strengths can work to your benefit, and sometimes to your detriment, you can begin leveraging that knowledge to your advantage. That's when things that appeared previously impossible begin to look like they can become reality.

Here's how it sounds when your signature strengths are finding traction in your work:

- "It feels like I'm on vacation! I'm getting paid, but I would already be doing much of this anyway. It's who I am."

- "I can't explain it! I have more energy, and things feel less stressful. It feels like I'm in my zone a lot more of the time."

- "I feel like I can contribute more when I'm operating in my strengths. It just makes me feel more like I'm helping others."

And here's what it sounds like when they aren't:

- "I've been in this role for three years now. It feels like I don't even know myself anymore, and it's eroding my confidence."

- "I feel like I have to be someone else to be successful in my job. It's weird because I can and I'm good at it, but it leaves me emotionally and physically exhausted."

13

Supportive People

Choose to focus your time, energy, and conversation
around people who inspire you, support you, and help you
to grow you into your happiest, strongest, wisest self.

KAREN SALMANSOHN

THERE'S AN old adage that's been repeated for as long as
I've been in the professional world: people don't leave jobs,
they leave bosses. In almost every study I've ever read about
why people leave their jobs, I've found some level of truth to
this clichéd wisdom. But what about the reverse? What makes
people stay?

The first time I was a leader who needed to fill some open
positions, I noticed a pattern in the responses of candidates I
was interviewing. Okay, let's be honest, I didn't notice it until
the answers hit me over the head again and again. Initially I had
started asking people why they were choosing to leave their current jobs. I got a wide range of answers, many of them reflecting
one of the seven elements of an ideal career, such as, "I'm not
growing," or, "I want to help people," for example. But I also
noticed that although some people had thought about leaving
their job for a long time, they hadn't left.

So I began asking why they hadn't left. Sometimes it was simply because they hadn't received an offer. But more often there was another reason. They would say, "I didn't want to leave the people," meaning their boss or their coworkers. Years later, I see this phenomenon constantly, and it's a daily conversation at HTYC.

Bosses and other people around you have a profound impact on whether or not you're thriving. We all know it fundamentally. But the question to ask is, What should you look for when it comes to the people side of your ideal career? There are three main areas that matter more than others for finding the right people to spend your time with daily. In this chapter, I'll discuss exactly what to look for, but first let's talk about something that is less obvious.

Social Systems Create Your Normal

In his book *Predictably Irrational: The Hidden Forces That Shape Our Decisions*, Duke University professor Dan Ariely writes, "We usually think of ourselves as sitting in the driver's seat, with ultimate control over the decisions we made and the direction our life takes; but, alas, this perception has more to do with our desires—with how we want to view ourselves—than with reality."[1]

Ariely points out that we are often a product of the systems we are plugged into, and specifically the accepted social norms of the people within those systems. This is worth considering because the impact of accepting a job offer comes with more far-reaching consequences than people realize. When you say yes to an offer, you're also saying yes to all of the social norms within that system.

So, if you are surrounded by people who think that working seventy-hour weeks is what is needed to be successful, you're going to default to working long hours in that environment.

When I worked in a french fry processing plant, it was par for the course to eat french fries in our meetings! Sounds great, right? Well, maybe, depending on whether you call daily french fries part of a healthy diet.

The Right Supportive People for Your Ideal Career

Now, let's consider a study conducted by Nicholas A. Christakis and James H. Fowler that evaluated how big an influence your social network is on you.[2] They analyzed the data set from one of the longest-running health studies ever. Using the data from 12,067 people over thirty-two years, they made some shocking discoveries. For example, if the study participants had a friend who became obese, they were 57 percent more likely to become obese themselves. If they had a spouse who became obese, they were 37 percent more likely to become obese. What's even more interesting is that if they had a friend who had a friend who was obese, they were likely to become obese, too.

This sounds like crazy talk! How could people you've never even met have an impact on your behaviors? The lesson to take away here is to be careful whom you let into your life on a regular basis, because the social and behavioral norms you plug yourself into matter more than you might realize. Here are some examples that are more positive and less obvious:

- What if you were surrounded by people who normalize putting their family first and feel comfortable leaving midday to spend time at their kids' school?

- What if you have a boss and team who allow you to openly discuss mistakes and failures without judgment?

- What if you were surrounded by people who contribute their time and money to causes they care about?

Aside from your family, or anyone else you live with, your coworkers are whom you spend the most time with. These are the people who will have an influence on your life behaviors. For this reason, it's critical to consider whom you want to be surrounded by, because if the people in your new opportunity don't believe in some of what you've identified as creating an ideal career for you and behave accordingly, it's unlikely the role will be a long-lived match.

In your ideal career, I encourage you to look for a boss, coworkers, and a leadership team who are supportive in two ways:

1   They help you with or support you in the other elements of your ideal career.

2   They create an environment where it's okay to be yourself, you're allowed to learn from mistakes, and you're challenged in positive and healthy ways.

Let's start with the first point. When I say that you need to find a boss, leaders, and coworkers who support you in the other elements of your ideal career, here's what I mean:

- If flexibility is the most important thing for you, you must work with people who normalize flexibility in the ways you need it.

- If you value creativity or growth, your boss must also value this.

- If you value using your strengths, you must first understand what they are and then make sure they align naturally with what is valuable to the people in that organization.

- If you want to contribute to the community that you live in, you'd better find a group of people who also care about that same community.

Is It Okay to Be Yourself?

Now, let's look at how important it is to have an environment where it's okay to simply be you.

"I feel like I have to be a different person at work."

I've heard this statement often during my many years working in HR, then later in operations, and now interacting with our clients at HTYC. Some of this can be explained by the fact that you're at rest when you're home, and it's likely you behave differently when you're in rest mode. But you shouldn't have to act like a different person when you are working. I'm not talking about being able to attend work in your pajamas (although I have done that from time to time on our HTYC team meetings). I'm also not talking about imposter syndrome, a concept one of my favorite authors, Seth Godin, has helped to normalize. This syndrome is expressed as a psychological pattern of doubt about our skills, talents, or accomplishments and a persistent internalized fear of being exposed as a fraud, despite external evidence of competence.[3]

Instead, I'm referring to when you feel you have to assume another identity and spend most of your day acting as though you're someone you're not. I've met countless highly accomplished and capable people who are simply surrounded by others who expect them to be a different person. But the impact of functioning for long periods of time as a "someone else" other than who you are may lead to severe consequences, including eroded confidence, depression, and even feeling like you don't know who you are or what you stand for anymore.

Remember Michael, the former finance executive from a top movie studio whose story I shared at the beginning of this book? Michael lost twenty pounds due to job-related stress, but the people around him appeared not to notice that he was struggling, or they simply didn't care. And I've seen much, much worse. This is what it looks like when you *don't* have supportive people in your work corner.

Another client, Dan, explained how supportive people in his workplace do accept him for who he is. He told me, "I'm great at what I do, and I'm also covered in tattoos. I don't have to hide who I am at work just because I have them, but I know that many organizations aren't open to that."

Having supportive people in your work is not just about being a freakin' awesome executive who also happens to have inked sleeves. At its heart, finding supportive people is about finding places where you can be more of who you are and whom you want to become. And, most importantly, a place where that support is enabled within the organization.

14

Values

I have learned that as long as I hold fast to my beliefs and
values—and follow my own moral compass—then
the only expectations I need to live up to are my own.

MICHELLE OBAMA

USED TO work for the corporate office of a franchised company (just one of my multiple careers). At one point my boss
asked me to collect a debt from a former franchise owner by
sitting outside of their current workplace and waiting for
them. It felt so, so wrong, like I was a mobster. As I sat there,
waiting nervously, I was thinking how out of alignment this felt
with my morals. When the former franchisee came out of her
workplace, she was mortified to see me.

Now, I highly value treating other people as equals. I also
highly value efficiency and maximization of time and money.
Most importantly, I value creating situations where everyone
wins. But that particular corporate environment created situations where I was asked to do things that were completely in
contrast with my values. Fast-forward: I didn't collect the money,
and later I found out that what I'd been asked to do amounted to

illegal debt collection. It was also a terrible use of my time for the modest amount of $2,000.

When your work reflects who you are as a person morally, ethically, and professionally, when you don't have to hide or compromise yourself to do your work, and when you are able to bring your complete self to your job, that's when you know your values are aligned with your role. If you are surrounded by people and an organization that aligns with what you value, stress is minimized.

But if that is not the case, things can quickly disintegrate to the point where you don't know who you are anymore. Putting yourself in this situation eats away at your soul and identity. The by-product of spending your time out of alignment with who you are and whom you want to be is severe. Eventually it erodes confidence.

Here's what real people say about having a misalignment with what they value most:

- "My company is not a cultural fit for me... although I am highly regarded, it's a terrible quality of life... I want to find something that allows me to be me, enjoy my whole life (have a life), not compromise my health and relationships. I want to work somewhere I can get behind their culture and their business and really thrive personally. No one at work knows how much I dislike it there. They think I'm doing great. It's pretense for me and there are no options to stay and thrive. I need to leave."

- "I am tired, physically and mentally, of what I am doing. Always being on and pushing my team to complete projects. Feeling like I am losing value as a person, always feeling like I am battling people. I no longer feel like I am helping people. Feel like this is a dead-end job, with limited upside. Wondering how long I can keep this up."

It's also the case that sometimes your values change, and sometimes the values of the company and the people around you change. Both these situations are normal, and it's okay to leave that situation if it's no longer a match for your values. This happened to me in one of my many career roles.

But first let's go back in time. Ever since I was a little kid, I used to wonder why adults never ran up the stairs. I mean, it was way fun. Why wouldn't people want to run up the stairs? One day someone took me aside and explained to me that when you become an adult you have less energy and you just don't want to run upstairs. I (of course) thought that was stupid. So, at seven years old, I resolved to continue running upstairs, and I did so even when I got a job in HR leadership at a food manufacturer (the same place where we ate french fries at every meeting).

For the first few years, I still ran up the stairs to my office. But then a new CEO came in, and I was told it was a safety risk and that, since I was on the leadership team, I needed to set an example. This may seem like a small—even silly—reason to leave a company, but it was symptomatic of a bigger change in my values. Around the same time, I also started taking a keen interest in my health. I eventually realized that, although many aspects of that company aligned with what I wanted, selling french fries didn't fit with how much I'd grown to value health.

Regardless of how you feel about fried potatoes, I would encourage you to take the time to understand what is most important for you, what you value above all else. If you're continuously supporting a product, growing a company, or working with people who are out of alignment with what you value most, that role is going to feel off at best and like you're selling a part of your soul at worst.

This is what it sounds like when your values are in alignment:

* "It feels like they get me here. I've finally found my people!"

- "There are people from all over the world in our organization. We all have different cultures and experiences, but we care about the same things, and that makes it feel like we're all going through it together. It's just easier."

And here is what it sounds like when your values are out of alignment with your work:

- "It seems almost like what I'm doing is wrong, like I'm supporting something that I don't really agree with."

- "It's hard to sell a product when you fundamentally disagree with what's happening at the top. I understand, but we clearly value different things."

15

Creating Your Ideal Career Profile

Success is the progressive
realization of a worthy ideal.

EARL NIGHTINGALE

T HTYC we use the Ideal Career Profile as our tool of choice for finding what would make up an ideal career opportunity for our clients. I invented it when I needed a way to represent what I had learned about my own version of an ideal career. If you use the seven elements of an ideal career as your guide, you'll find that you have the start of a blueprint for your own extraordinary career.

Here's how it works: the ICP helps you determine the characteristics that are most important to you in each of the seven elements that make up meaningful work. This helps you create an overall picture of what you really need from your career. Think about it as your ideal career checklist.

You'll notice in the graphic that an ICP is broken into two sections for each of the seven elements. This is because

MINIMUMS: MUST-HAVES TO BE AT MY BEST	IDEALS: WHAT WOULD BE EXTRAORDINARY
CONTRIBUTION	
☐ The work matters—I must care about the "what" we are doing	☐ Work with small, tight-knit groups 50 percent of the time
☐ Have a voice with leadership and use it to drive positive change	☐ Continue working with market trends, patterns, paradigm shifts
FLEXIBILITY AND AUTONOMY	
☐ Be able to work in office or remotely—my choice	☐ Take three weeks off each year for overseas travel
QUALITY OF LIFE	
☐ Earn $127K per year to support investing/savings/travel goals	☐ Ownership opportunity (equity/stock/partnership)
☐ Do activities multiple times a week that take 100 percent of my attention and cognitive ability (e.g., yoga)	☐ Family balance matters—I want more of the time I've had this year with kids/home
GROWTH	
☐ Have the ability to be creative to solve problems	☐ Must be an organization with a built-in mentorship network
SIGNATURE STRENGTHS	
☐ Use my communication and strategic abilities to share ideas, help people understand new concepts	☐ A culture that enables everyone to use their unique strengths to do what they enjoy doing
SUPPORTIVE PEOPLE	
☐ Must be a culture where it's okay to make mistakes and ideas are rewarded	☐ Work with people who are incredibly talented, intelligent, and I enjoy spending time with
VALUES	
☐ Must be a company where being a good parent is normalized	☐ Be ridiculously helpful and take care of others

we've observed over the years that many people have a difficult time focusing on ideals if they haven't first identified their minimums—the must-haves or "deal breakers." Once the line is drawn in the sand, it becomes easier to think much bigger.

We've also noticed another challenge. So many people say, "I can't do this because some of these are so intertwined." They can't decide what's important to them because the elements appear to depend on each other. For example, some people say, "I would take less money if I had more flexibility." This seems like a reasonable statement. It may also be true for the many people who've said it to me. Let's evaluate it, though. What goes into that seemingly innocent statement?

First, why do you believe you would have to take less money? Based on the people we help every day at HTYC, this is not true. Second, when you make that kind of statement, you are assuming there must be a trade-off: you can only have this if you let go of that. But being paid a premium to tolerate a lack of what you really need (flexibility) isn't thriving. It is settling, which is the exact opposite of the reason you're creating a profile of your ideal career. The reason to go through all the time, effort, and energy to identify what you're willing to accept in your life and target what is ideal for you in your career is not to figure out what you are willing to trade off or give up. It's an opportunity to create a vision of a career that truly fits your life. The point is to begin your search with the ideal end in mind.

Happen To Bonus

Go to happentoyourcareer.com/bonus to download an example of an Ideal Career Profile with your book bonuses.

Easy to Say Yes, Harder to Say No

At HTYC we believe that the best indicator of how successful we are is that our clients are receiving and turning down good opportunities before they eventually accept one that fits them best. That's what the Ideal Career Profile does for you. It brings together all the micro-decisions you've made about what you need in your career and how your career impacts other areas of your life and allows you to make great decisions for yourself when the time arises. More importantly, it allows you to make more intentional decisions instead of reactive decisions you might regret later.

If you've ever gone to the grocery store without a list while you're feeling hungry, you know how hard it is to make good decisions in the moment. You end up coming back with Cool Ranch Doritos and double fudge ice cream, and then you eat all the ice cream and tell your family it's better that they don't have ice cream in the freezer to taunt them (okay, maybe that's just me).

REACTIVE DECISIONS

Decisions you make in the moment based on what you're feeling	e.g., accepting the first job you're offered

INTENTIONAL DECISIONS

Decisions you make carefully based on knowledge and preparation	e.g., identifying what you want in a job and then finding it

When you've made all the smaller decisions about what you need in your career in advance, when the time comes, you'll be a lot less likely to come home with the Doritos-and-ice-cream equivalent to work. Exciting and tasty at first, but then you're paying for that decision in many more ways than just at the checkout.

It's easy to say no to opportunities that are a terrible fit (well, maybe not ice cream). But it's harder to say no to good opportunities. The biggest challenge in that situation is the allure of those good opportunities. You can see the potential in them, but they aren't freakin' amazing. This is when you need a clear understanding of what you want and need from your work so you are confident in what is right for you. But you also need the courage to say no to a good, but not great, opportunity, even when you're scared the great opportunity isn't going to come along and you might have missed out on the good one.

Think about this for a moment:

> Good is not the same as extraordinary.
> Good is the same as average.
> Average usually equals mediocre.
> Mediocrity is not thriving.

I once had a client who looked at the Ideal Career Profile and said, "That's just like a filter!" Exactly: you can run decisions through your ICP and see which ones filter out on the other side. The real benefit of creating a profile of your ideal career is that, by making all your specific decisions in advance, you only need to ask one simple question when an opportunity presents itself:

Does this opportunity bring me closer to my ideals?

If the career opportunity makes it through your ICP filter, then you can consider it further. If it doesn't hit your ideals as it makes its way through the ICP filter, then you know you don't have to keep exploring that opportunity, deliberating for hours, and wasting time on it when you should be looking for that great opportunity.

Even though this type of reflective evaluation is a cornerstone of finding the ideal career opportunity, the ICP is not what moves you into a new career. After you've done all this work, you've generated a hypothesis of your ideal career and life. But even though it's a highly educated guess, it's still just a guess. Before you spend time and effort making your career change, take some steps to make sure you're going to want to work in it. I don't want you to get to your new role and company and realize that only the names and faces have changed and you've made a totally wrong move. That's no good for you or the people you might be working with!

So, how do you avoid that? You test your hypothesis, your ideal career, through experiments. In the next chapter, you'll learn exactly why the most common question in all of career history is also the most misguided.

Happen To Checklist

Answer these questions:

- [ ] What does extraordinary look like for you?

- [ ] Where in your life have you already reached your version of extraordinary that you want to keep in place?

- [ ] Where are you missing your version of extraordinary right now?

Happen To Bonus

Go to happentoyourcareer.com/8day to get access to our "Figure It Out" mini-course. You'll receive a daily email with exercises that will help you begin identifying your ideal career.

PART FOUR

MAKING IT HAPPEN

16

Designing Career Experiments

Good things happen when you meet strangers.

YO-YO MA

WHEN I was sixteen years old, I was hit upside the head with the world's most misguided question. The question was, and I'm sure you were asked it, too,

"Have you decided what you want to do?"

Well, like many young people, I had no clue how to answer this question. But I did know one thing: I badly wanted to participate in adulty things. So if jumping blindly into something was what adults did—so I assumed—maybe I could just pick something? At the time I loved playing guitar and bass, but I knew that musicians traveled constantly to promote their music. I didn't want to do that, so being in a band was out. But I loved music. Maybe I could work for a recording studio? Yes, I was totally adulting hard!

Age seventeen rolled around. As I began answering that original misguided question with my "studio recording" answer, I was met with another question. "So, where are you going to study studio recording?" I didn't know. I thought that I would just practice it and figure it out. But everyone seemed to think I needed to go to college to study studio recording. Unfortunately, there weren't many studio recording programs available at the time, and the tuition fees for the few I did find cost about five times my community college budget.

That's okay, I thought. I could blindly pick something else! Now I was going into computer science with a backup plan in music theory. During college I changed majors nine times, eventually making my experience a full year longer than average (yes, I was a super senior). At the time, I had no idea what a huge advantage this gave me. By swinging from major to major, I was exposed to a wide variety of classes and subject areas. I learned that I didn't enjoy writing code for hours on end. I also learned that there are people who are responsible for entire computer network systems in companies. That knowledge led me to shift into a business program, where I became exposed to marketing, human resources, management, and finance.

Spending a little longer in college to try many areas ended up saving me years because I gained exposure and valuable feedback about what I liked, disliked, and loved. I didn't love writing code in a closet, but I did love solving business problems using human psychology.

Why Career Experiments Are a Great Investment

It was fifteen years after my college experience before I fully realized just how valuable all that exposure and experimentation was. At this point in time I was having lots of conversations in which people told me, "I thought that if I switched companies that would solve the problem," or, "I've been considering a career change for years, but it seemed like such a risk." The light went on, and I began to understand just how important exposure and experimentation are when you are deciding about what you want to do, no matter where you are in your career.

Then I thought, What if there was a way to figure out what you really wanted without having to commit years to staying with another company that potentially wasn't a fit? What if you didn't have to wonder anymore about how to go about finding your ideal career without taking huge risks?

Well, you don't have to wonder. The best way to find out is to spend some time up front to get your answers. You don't need to make a full change to a new industry to find out that what you wanted had nothing to do with the industry. This chapter lays out a methodology for finding an opportunity that fits—without taking such huge risks. The key tool for doing this is career experiments.

HTYC has helped clients run countless experiments over the years doing just about anything that you can imagine. Here are some examples.

- Eric created a blog about solar energy projects and contacted CEOs and other experts in the solar industry for their comments to use in his articles. This forced him to learn about focused areas of solar energy while simultaneously building relationships with people in the industry.

- Rena took on a short-term freelance consulting gig to find out if she liked paid consulting.

- Celena quit her job so she could make space in her life to find what did fit her. She started a podcast and took advantage of multiple opportunities that didn't require all her time.

- Bowe got his Merchant Mariner Credential so he could take part in an at-sea apprenticeship and test his assumptions about a larger "at-sea life."

Career experiments can be wide ranging. Not everyone needs to get a Merchant Mariner Credential or develop a website. And not everyone should quit their job or pursue freelance work. Career experiments must also be customized to you and your life situation, and some experiments tend to help you more than others. Not all experiments are created equal, but there are some commonalities between great experiments.

What Makes a Great Career Experiment

One of our clients, Adam Bloom, told me that experiments should be like rock climbing. I didn't have a clue what he meant. Adam explained by telling me about a college buddy of his who loved rock climbing. "He used to take me to the climbing gym. Once in a while, I would make it to the top of the climbing wall. My friend wasn't impressed. Other times, I'd fall. I'd be dangling in the air from a rope harness, shouting profanities in frustration, but those were the climbs my friend got excited about. Mostly because he liked to laugh at me, but also because, as he said, 'If you're not falling, you're not trying.'"

Career experiments should be like that—some of them should fail. You should be pushing yourself past what you know you can do and exploring possibilities you're not sure about. Don't just do the experiments you know will work—that won't teach you anything. Do the ones that feel uncertain. When some of your experiments fail, that's okay! Maybe you'll take a contract gig and it won't work out. Great! Finding out what you don't like is just as important as finding out what you do like. Maybe you chat with people in a certain industry and don't connect with them. Did you chat with lawyers and find them boring? Did you chat with talent agents and find them obnoxious? Terrific news! Now you can save the time, energy, and suffering of getting a job alongside those people, finding out you don't like them, and ending up as miserable as you were in your previous career.

Some of the career experiments that you expect to fail may even succeed, and you will discover something new about yourself. These are the best kind, because they potentially open up a new avenue of experiments on your journey to realizing a truly ideal career.

Career experiments have a few specific benefits:

- **A career experiment is an action.** It takes you out of the realm of thinking about doing something and makes you do it. Change is measurable in actions, and a career experiment is a great way to take action toward your goal of changing careers. And taking one action makes taking the next action easier, building momentum toward your larger career-change goals.

- **A career experiment allows you to test a specific career hypothesis.** Maybe you are working for a big company and you believe a smaller company would be better. Maybe you'd like to write more, or work in human resources, or join a startup. Now's your chance to give it a shot. Your Ideal Career Profile will have a list of different elements. They sound good, but you won't know if they actually work for you until you try them out. Career experiments are a way to do that.

- **Career experiments are a great way to confront your fears about career change.** Rather than trying things that are new, try things that feel uncomfortable or are likely to fail. A good career experiment should be an experiment in the truest sense of the word, meaning that you don't know what the outcome will be.

But a good career experiment should also be a multi-benefit activity. You don't want career-experiment pasta that is only made of starch. You want career-experiment superfoods—think spinach and garlic and turmeric!—that provide lots of different benefits. These career experiments allow you to test several career hypotheses. This isn't about testing multiple things at once. It's about strategically choosing experiments that move you further along in your career change journey once you've completed it.

For example, let's say that I identify two people whom I've never met before in industries that I believe I'm very interested in. I decide that I'm going to do the speed-dating version of job shadowing with them. Both people say yes. Everything goes well, and I learn that I'm interested in both industries. And if those people also have the authority to help or hire me, now I have the benefit of starting new relationships with people who are in my industry. Maybe those same people can even introduce me to other people in their industry. Kapow! One short experiment, but with multiple benefits!

Career Experiment Guidelines

When designing career experiments, you'll need to consider these guidelines:

- **Use your Ideal Career Profile as a guide.** When you design a career experiment, start with what you know. What do you want from your next job? Use your ICP as a guide. Start with your highest priorities and be selfish. Put everyone else's wants and needs in a box for now. For just a moment, stop worrying about your spouse, your kids, your mortgage broker, your book club, your student lender. This isn't their career, it's yours.

* **Leverage your signature strengths.** Playing to your strengths will make your experiments more likely to succeed (yes, you want some of your experiments to fail, but not all of them). An experiment may also give you an opportunity to take advantage of strengths that were underutilized in your previous career. A great experiment will provide feedback on whether something scratches an itch as an outlet for your strengths.

* **Try on a new work persona.** If you've previously been the person who keeps to themself at the office, maybe you want to try being more outgoing. What response do you get from your colleagues? Or maybe you always thought you'd enjoy hard-core data analysis with intense pivot tables, macros, and spreadsheets for miles. I thought that. I created some opportunities to "be that person." Spoiler alert: I did not enjoy it. Get some feedback. You're bound to learn more about yourself and what makes you fulfilled at work. Doing work that favors your strengths will also build your confidence as you continue to home in on your ideal career.

Here is a list of additional criteria I use to help me assess whether an experiment is a great one:

* Does it test your hypothesis (aka the assumptions on your Ideal Career Profile)?

* When the experiment is finished, could it move you closer to an opportunity than when you started? Does it position you to move faster when you make a decision about your career direction?

* Does it leverage your signature strengths?

* Does it serve you and your goals?

- Does it work with where you're at, meaning the time and situation you are in currently? An experiment that won't work for your situation is just wishful thinking.

- Is the experiment focused on the long term?

Following these guidelines doesn't mean the experiments will always be easy (although sometimes they can be). But some experiments, we've found, are slightly easier than others and have potentially bigger payoffs. These types of experiments are the ones we find ourselves recommending most often.

HTYC's Four Most Common Experiments

Although there are infinite possibilities around how to conduct an experiment, four types of experiments are more common because they are highly effective:

1　The Social Goldilocks
2　The Volunteer
3　The Paid Researcher
4　The Helpful Opportunist

I want to share a specific example of each type so that you can see which ones might apply to your world (and which ones don't), but first, it's important to acknowledge that experiments don't provide job offers. A well-designed experiment will move you further along in the process once you decide to proceed forward, but these experiments themselves are separate from the process of getting a real, live paying opportunity or job offer. This idea that you're experimenting for the purpose of identifying and validating what is right for you may be challenging, but I promise that you'll learn a great deal about what your ideal career opportunity looks like.

Now, let's have a look at these experiments.

1. The Social Goldilocks

Laura Morrison was bored. Her current role no longer offered the challenge she was looking for. What she didn't know was whether the unique type of challenge she wanted was in product management, marketing, user research, or any other areas she was considering. Furthermore, she wasn't totally sure what type of organization would support the challenge she was looking for. How could she find out?

She started by searching for "best places to work in Boston." She identified a few companies she thought she might be interested in. Laura chose several roles she thought might fit her ICP (product management, user research, product marketing). She then identified people in those organizations who had already worked or were currently working in these areas. Next, she reached out to those people and had short conversations with them to learn more about them and those types of roles.

The beauty of this experiment is that it works much the same way it did when Goldilocks tried all the chairs and all the beds and tasted the porridge in all the bowls. She learned that some were too hard, were too soft, or tasted too much like porridge. She also learned that some things were just right. This contact- and conversation-driven experiment quickly allowed Laura to learn about a variety of roles and to remove options from consideration that weren't a fit. Through this experiment, she eliminated user research and focused her attention on product management at one company in particular: The Predictive Index.

This was not an overnight process, though. It took Laura several months and twenty-plus conversations with fifteen different people. She spent time getting introductions from friends, having conversations, reaching out to people she had never met, and asking a million questions along the way. Even though each conversation was about the other person's experience, it allowed Laura to learn more about herself and what resonated with her. She would ask questions like, "What makes you good at what you do?" and "What are the downsides to your role?" She told me later that this approach, which was so outside of her comfort zone at the time, forced her to become more curious and even shaped how she would interact with people as a product manager who needs to be an expert in posing questions with curiosity. Most importantly, developing this skill set for experimenting helped her to learn what she wanted to do next.

When Laura decided that The Predictive Index was the company she really was interested in working with, she then had a huge competitive advantage compared to anyone else who wanted to work for that company. She had a relationship with multiple people there who could help or even hire her. This meant she didn't have to apply through the website. She didn't get stalled by gatekeepers. Instead, she could just pick up the phone and ask, "What would it take for me to work here in the future?"

She didn't pick up the phone, though; instead, she sent this email to one of the VPs she had built a relationship with:

> Thank you again for our conversation this week! It was really exciting to hear about PI as a product and the boundless opportunities for using the assessment to improve human interactions. Your passion is clear and infectious.
>
> After getting off the phone with you earlier this week and then diving in with James to understand my personal assessment, I found myself really excited to explore what working with you could mean. I would love the opportunity to talk with you again next week to let you know what I'm thinking about. Tuesday afternoon, Wednesday morning, or Friday morning would work best for me. Let me know if you have fifteen minutes to spare.
>
> Have a great weekend!
>
> Best,
> Laura

P.S. I would love to have the plaque you described with PI insights hanging in my team's cubicles!

This led to a conversation with the VP, which led to more conversations in which Laura and The Predictive Index team had serious discussions about what would be the right role for her in the company. Ultimately, she received a job offer in product management without even going through the company's "normal" hiring process.

2. The Volunteer

When I was considering leaving Target after spending four years in HR, I was unsure if I wanted to stay in HR or move into another role. But I needed to find out without taking half a year to do it. Alyssa and I had just had our second kid, and we were attempting to get in shape by training for a half marathon. So, I decided I was going to volunteer my way to finding the answer.

After going to a few events with the local chapter of the Society for Human Resources Management, I asked how I could help. The thing about volunteer-driven organizations is they are always strapped for volunteers. My offer of help quickly turned into a seat on the board and helping to run events.

Now, this was not my first career change and certainly not my first experiment, so I knew that part of what I wanted from this experience was to meet as many people as I possibly could. I could then learn more about them and their jobs and build new relationships, which could lead to additional help once I actually decided where I wanted to be!

Stephanie Bilbrey did the same thing. She volunteered for a local marketing group and got exposure to a wide variety of marketing roles. She also learned—wait for it—that she didn't like marketing. Okay, she liked some parts of the industry, but what she thought might be the solution for her next career change was absolutely not "go deeper into marketing."

This was valuable insight for her because, after multiple job changes, she didn't want to continue to find temporary solutions. This insight alone saved her one additional career change. As an extra benefit, the relationships she built in the marketing group led to a copywriting contract gig that helped to tide her over when she was between jobs.

But does your experimentation require that you constantly offer your services for free? Stephanie's other experiments prove that you don't have to.

3. The Paid Researcher

When Stephanie was working for a community college, she found that she loved the people and the work environment, even though she was still struggling with identifying what type of work might be right for her. Through her experiment volunteering with the local marketing group, she knew it wasn't marketing.

She had other ideas up her sleeve, though. She decided that she was going to volunteer in a completely different way. She got wind of a committee being formed to re-evaluate internal communication at the college. She had a sneaking suspicion she might love this work, and what better way to find out than by doing it while she was already getting paid. She joined the committee and got to experience firsthand the responsibility of improving communication for the employees of the college. Now, to be clear, this position did require some extra hours, but the benefit was that Stephanie was actively experimenting in a way that was good for her and her employer. At HTYC, we call this form of experimentation the "paid researcher."

Stephanie and the committee improved the college's internal communications by consolidating channels and developing simple criteria to streamline communications. For Stephanie, this was the first time she'd felt an intrinsic reward from work in a sustaining and meaningful way. When she was writing a script for a video, it scratched her itch for fun. When she was talking with other people about communication problems, challenges, and potential solutions, she was geeking out while others were saying, "How can you even talk about this?"

What's important to note is that Stephanie needed to run multiple small experiments (volunteering and paid research) to get these breakthroughs. By choosing the experiments she did, she got more than just the breakthroughs, though. They gave her valuable experience that allowed her to be seriously considered for roles she really wanted in internal communication later on.

James Sannan did something similar. He was employed at one of the world's largest aerospace companies, where he started to work with software development technologies in a business-focused role. He found that he was fascinated by how other tech companies were designing these products. At this time, he also thought that he might be interested in big tech. He used the opportunity to learn more about how big tech companies like Amazon operate. This micro-experiment gave him the necessary information to do his current job more effectively, but also enough feedback to realize that he had a great appreciation for those tech organizations. He knew that Amazon would be a good organization for him, so after the company initially turned him down for a role, he persisted until he got the right job offer.

Kristy Wenz, who, you might recall from earlier, created a role for herself in wine and travel, did paid research too. She knew that she wanted to try doing more writing and took on several paid writing gigs. She learned that she did want to write, and particularly about wine and travel. But she also learned that she loved some of the operations and communications experiences she'd had in the past. She had to have all three. Now she knew with certainty where she'd like to be spending her time.

It took Kristy a month or two, but she realized that one of the companies she was already writing for could benefit from the exact combination of skills and experiences she was looking for. Plus, it was exactly the type of environment she wanted, a startup where she could work directly with the owner. She had an initial conversation with the owner and asked if he might find the idea of a chief communications officer beneficial to the company. He did, and that interest quickly turned into a serious conversation as Kristy continued to ask questions about what they might need.

Fast-forward multiple conversations and many weeks later, and Kristy went from experimenting to creating her own role at a company that had no existing budget for such a role. This type of unicorn opportunity is an impossible feat for those who are unwilling to do the prerequisite work of getting clear on what they want, testing it out, and putting themselves in position to achieve (nearly) impossible feats.

Kristy's, James's, and Stephanie's stories all have similarities in that they leveraged an existing paid relationship with an organization. But this isn't the only way to do "paid research" experiments. Over the years, we've helped many of our clients do consulting gigs, freelance work, contract jobs, bridge roles, and many other paid opportunities with the dual purpose of being paid while facilitating an experiment. But, although the paid researcher is one of my favorite experiments, there's still one more we need to look at.

4. The Helpful Opportunist

Mike was an engineer who lived in Portland, Oregon. He found himself needing to make a career change when his wife took a job in Seattle, Washington. Mike needed to find a new job while applying, making connections, and interviewing remotely. But he also didn't want to accept just any job. Mike wanted to make the move to leadership at the same time.

"I know how to get introduced to people and talk to folks. I've done this remote job search thing a few times. What was going to make it different for me, though, is that it's an opportunity to change not just location but also position." The question was, What industry and which companies were right for him? And how could he test this quickly while searching remotely from another state?

For Mike, a career transition wasn't just about finding a job but about finding the right place for himself in a new community while also showing people that he was there for more than just a job. He realized that having a broader focus in his search was necessary and required effort and a sense of vulnerability.

Mike knew this could be a big undertaking, and the best way to get going would be to start by making it as easy as possible. He asked friends if they knew people where he wanted to work, and then asked them about their experience or if they could introduce him to people. The most important thing Mike realized is that, to set himself apart, he needed to bring value to the people and organizations he was talking to: "It's not about what I can do, but what problems are being faced." He created a systematic approach to take advantage of the short, remote conversations he was able to have with potential employers. He found organizations and positions that he thought might be a good fit. Then he sought ways to talk with people in those organizations, and when he did so, he asked them what they needed. He made sure to connect with his contacts after their meetings, touching on points from the conversation.

Mike used an approach similar to Laura's by having as many conversations as he could in the industry he thought he wanted. Then he became the "helpful opportunist." During a meeting with a potential employer, he would ask them what business obstacles they were struggling with. What big-vision questions were they wrestling with? What impact did they want to make over the next five years? What would make their life easier?

Then Mike went away from that meeting to come up with solutions and did this unsolicited, unpaid, just for fun.

How did he do this exactly? During the initial conversations, Mike would hear someone say, "I have this need," or, "I need to solve this." He would then ask follow-up questions to learn exactly what was most important and why. Then he would go and create a spreadsheet, a piece of code or equation, and follow up. Here's how that follow-up conversation would go: "Remember that problem we talked about? I've thought about it and created this as a solution for you for free. Enjoy!"

When you are a hiring manager and meet with someone who listened so well and is so excited about the work you are doing that they do the work unsolicited and then offer it to you, that says exciting things about the potential contribution that person can make if you bring them into your team.

No surprise, then, that this experiment of being a helpful opportunist worked ridiculously well for two reasons: First, Mike was able to test-drive and experience the work firsthand and decide if it was something he had further interest in (the experiment part of the experiment!). And second, almost nobody does this, so it made him stand out from the crowd in the minds of his potential future employers. More importantly, he learned through the experiments that there were some types of work and some companies he simply didn't enjoy, saving himself potentially years by helping him narrow down his list (the opposite of taking huge career risks).

Throughout this experiment, Mike ended up building relationships with many people he had an interest in working with. Later this resulted in interviews and, ultimately, several job offers that put him over six figures for the first time in his life.

Giving Up Your Attachment to (Ice Cream) Outcomes

The challenge for many people when it comes to experimenting is that you really do need to give up your emotional attachment to the outcome for it to fully succeed. Career experiments must be about validating and finding what's right for you. Only when you approach it that way will you get to answers. This part of the process is about exploring, not getting to a job as fast as you can. This is the time to intentionally seek good answers that will save you time for many years down the road. The wonderful reward of doing these experiments well is that they often give you a competitive advantage, which allows you to achieve results differently than if you simply walked in off the street or applied online for various jobs.

Laura was able to bypass the normal application process and get an increase in salary from $120K to $132K. Stephanie was able to learn what she was the best at, which allowed her to present herself differently in interviews and ultimately almost double her previous salary. James was able to change industries when other people were telling him he was silly to even think it was possible.

But you cannot expect that every experiment you design will lead to these types of outcomes. Remember that Kristy had multiple writing gigs that did not lead to anything other than feedback and information. Laura talked to plenty of people who had no connection to the role she ended up accepting. Most of the time, what you will get out of an experiment is a better understanding of what you need. But when you do get enough information, validation, and feedback to declare a direction for yourself, you'll be much further along than everyone else. You'll be in a better position to negotiate later, and you'll know that you're heading in the right direction for you!

Along the way there will be bumps in the road. Some- times those bumps will be more like volcanoes spewing lava everywhere. One thing I've learned is that every single person who makes career change a priority will experience setbacks on their way to becoming a Happy High Achiever. So, when all these setbacks happen, how do you work through them, and how do you keep going? Anticipating where and how those setbacks will arrive and what you can actually do about them is what we will cover in the next chapter.

Happen To Checklist

Answer these questions:

☐ How do you see career experiments benefiting you in your career change?

☐ What's one thing you learned from this chapter that you could apply immediately?

Happen To Bonus

Visit happentoyourcareer.com/bonus for additional ideas on experiments.

17

Adjusting to Setbacks

Everything will be okay in the end.
If it's not okay, it's not the end.
ATTRIBUTED TO JOHN LENNON

WAS INTRODUCED to Adam Bloom several years after his partner, Stacy, wrote an article for Citibank featuring Happen to Your Career. Adam was a lawyer who had been attempting to exit lawyer land for over a decade. He wanted to write, and he found that his unique combination of strategic and observational strengths was a huge asset. He also had a law degree and many years of experience, and he had even started his own firm.

My team began working with him, and he did a fantastic job of experimenting to learn what he really wanted. In one of his experiments, he landed a copywriting job with a startup that combined tech and law. This seemed like the perfect combination for Adam and even led to a full-time offer. Only it wasn't perfect, because the role needed some changes to make it align with the minimums that Adam had declared on his Ideal Career Profile.

As Adam started to negotiate with the startup, he learned more about the company, the leaders, and what his future opportunities or limitations would look like if he landed there. The idea of the perfect fit started to crumble, and it was apparent that this was not going to be the spot where Adam landed. As further evidence that this wasn't an environment with clear communication and an opportunity for Adam, the startup withdrew the offer in a knee-jerk reaction to his concerns and requests.

It was definitely the right move. Adam could see it. We at HTYC could see it, and even the company could see it. But in that moment, it felt like everything Adam was working on fell apart and he was back at square one, a big setback.

Don't worry, Adam did successfully transition from being a lawyer to a content strategist, but his experience with setbacks is a common occurrence for people looking for new careers. Almost every person we've ever worked with has experienced setbacks and has had to adjust their plan along the way. Setbacks can occur in two ways, but a common one is that you discover you need to move down a different path from what you were anticipating.

Reaching the Twenty-Third Mile

Remember Stephanie Bilbrey from the previous chapter? At one point she thought that marketing was the answer for her. She experimented with marketing and realized that this was not it, which required her to pivot and explore something else. You'll also recall that another experiment she did was to become part of an organization-wide committee to assess internal communications at the college she worked at. Although these are two sentences in this book, the two experiments represented many months of work on Stephanie's part in real life. Think about that for a moment: you just spent months working on an experiment to get to the realization that you don't want to do the thing you thought you might want to do.

Don't worry! That's a great place to be, because you've probably saved yourself years of going down the wrong path. And, more importantly, it allows you to stop pursuing that option and focus your attention on what you do want to be spending your time on for your career. This was true for Stephanie. She was able to stop pursuing marketing as an option. She also learned about communication through the lens of marketing, which led her to believe she might love internal comms or communication strategy.

Still, when these setbacks are happening in real time, it often doesn't feel like you are saving yourself years of work. For the many people my team has coached, instead of these moments feeling like wonderful pivotal milestones full of useful insight, they usually feel like everything is falling apart.

How could the feelings of this experience be so different from the impact of the experience itself?

Consider the marathoner's experience. My mom is a long-time runner. She's qualified for and run the Boston Marathon and has more marathon medals than she knows what to do with. She told me that the hardest part of running a marathon is around mile twenty-three: "All the excitement has worn off, and your body is starting to turn on you and you just want to be done already." In so many ways, you've already done the hardest work—all the training that led up to it, plus more than 80 percent of the race. As my mom describes it, "You're so close and yet so tired . . . you go through a lot of emotion when you get fatigued."

That's the mental place so many people get to in their career change. You're just ready to be done. So, when an experiment doesn't work, it doesn't always feel like this wonderful gift from the heavens. How, then, do you deal with this?

Well, as it turns out, if you've been reading this book, you've already planned for this! Remember your plan for inevitable success? That plan is important in the process to becoming a Happy High Achiever, but it becomes critical when you start experiencing setbacks either real or perceived. Whatever you've included on your plan now kicks into action and will be fully tested. Your accountability partner, friends, mentors, and coaches you've hired all come into play right about now. How does this play out in reality?

When people embark down the career-change path to Happy High Achiever, they often don't realize they will need to steer clear of "good job offers" and opportunities. Most people believe that all the work they are doing will lead to a single opportunity.

Mel received a job offer in human resources after many months. It wasn't at all what she wanted: the pay was about $40K too low, and it wasn't in an area she was excited about, but there was one key factor that got her attention. It was available to her right then and there. Yes, it was part of the plan for her career change to take another month or two. Yes, she had done all of this great work to define what she wanted to do. But this was not it. So, what did she do?

I can't tell you the number of times the coaches on my team and I have needed to step in to help our clients gracefully turn down job offers or opportunity conversations that are simply a distraction on the way to what they really want. This sounds like it shouldn't be a challenge, but remember, everything gets harder when you're in the twenty-third mile. You're no longer seeing things the same way. What you see is that there is a sure thing, an offer, that will end it all right now.

In Mel's case, she was worried about whether there would be another offer soon or at all. This made her fearful. And fear makes you do pretty crazy things. If fear is leading your decisions about what you accept and don't accept in your life, you will always find yourself settling and never thriving.

I coached Mel to turn down that job offer, and then we recalibrated her plan so that she could carry on her search for her ideal career. I can say with certainty that at that moment she did not believe me when I told her this would be a good move for her. However, less than six weeks later, Mel received not one but three additional offers! Two of them aligned beautifully with her Ideal Career Profile. But if Mel had not had a plan for inevitable success, and if she hadn't trusted that original plan that allowed her to finish the race, she would never, ever have gotten past that twenty-third mile.

Hitting the Skill Wall

The second common setback that can happen is when you hit a brick wall in the career-change process because you don't yet have the skills.

When I say "don't yet have the skills," you might think I'm referring to the skills needed for the job or occupation you want. Nope. Instead, I'm referring to the skills you will need to acquire to make your change or create the opportunity you're looking for.

This particular brick wall is devious. Not only does it usually pop up multiple times along the way, but when you experience this type of setback in the twenty-third mile, it feels like its own special kind of hell. It seems hopeless and like you've "tried everything" when it happens. The bottom line is that everyone we work with at HTYC hits this wall during their career change, but it does show up differently for everyone.

Vicky Meng worked in finance for years. She had a variety of experiences but really wanted to go into treasury. Spoiler alert: she made it to her ideal career! However, it took longer than she'd hoped, and there were not just one but two very low points when she didn't want to keep going.

I wish that I could tell you it was easy for Vicky. It was not. I wish that I could tell you that everything she did during her change worked well. Not even close. But that's the most compelling part of Vicky's whole story.

I spoke with Vicky after she made a career change into treasury, and she told me a story about the email that transformed her life in just one year. So, what did she actually do to get there? What caused her to have those low points when she wanted to give up? And how the heck did she move past the lows? Let's look at Vicky's journey as a timeline first so you can get a sense of how it progressed.

- **December:** Vicky decides she's no longer going to tolerate her current job and career direction.

- **January:** She sends me an email with "conversation" in the subject line, to kickstart her career change.

- **February:** She begins identifying her strengths, most useful experiences, skills, and assets, and she selects the coach she wants to work with for the rest of her journey.

- **March to May:** Vicky believes she wants to work in treasury. She spends three months conducting experiments, building relationships, and getting interviews.

- **June:** She gets an offer, but her coach convinces her to turn it down because it's not in alignment with her Ideal Career Profile. Vicky does this reluctantly.

- **July:** She hits her first low point. She was having success reaching people, but now it's happening more slowly. She feels like she is not making progress, which is especially hard to navigate because she just turned down an opportunity.

- **August to September:** Vicky realizes she's been doing what she feels she's "supposed to" (moving to San Francisco to get into treasury for tech), instead of pursuing what she really wants (staying in LA and pursuing her interests in treasury).

* **October:** She hits a second low point. By reaching out in unique and relevant ways, she is getting pushed to the front of the line for interviews for her ideal roles, but she is still not getting offers in treasury.

Even though Vicky had a ton of success reaching and meeting people (and was even offered a job), she had hit a brick wall. Emotionally she felt like she was back at square one. Hitting this wall meant that Vicky needed to move beyond her existing skills—what she already knows—to make her change. Here's why and how she overcame this setback.

Vicky felt like she didn't have enough specialized experience in any one area, which colored how she talked about herself during interviews. She would say, "I don't have very much experience in any one area, but I've worked in a lot of areas." Unfortunately, the interviewers adopted this opinion of her, too: she's great, but she just doesn't have much experience. But this couldn't have been further from the truth!

We began talking about her experience and looking at it differently using this statement as an example: "I have over five years' experience in cash flow, treasury, and financial analysis."

Do you see the difference in those two statements?

Vicky doesn't have a problem with having enough experience. Nope. Her challenge is how to present her unique experience in a way that's helpful to other organizations and leads her closer to what she wants.

Here's another example. Vicky would say, "I want to make a move to treasury," as if she had zero treasury experience, which was not helpful to her interviewers (and just plain not true). Instead, I suggested that she phrase her experience this way:

"What I would really love to do is take my unique experiences in treasury, cash flow, and analysis (and my big-picture exposure to all financial areas) and use that to specialize in treasury for a larger organization."

Once she started framing her experience this way, her ideal job offer arrived less than thirty days later.

Here's what most people miss during their search for an ideal career: it's a process! In Vicky's case, it wasn't just that she had to learn how to present her existing experiences differently. It wasn't that she had to turn down her job offer. Or that she had to go through low points and setbacks. It wasn't any one thing. It was all of it. Together.

Every single person we get to help go through a career change to their ideal career, not just the next job, goes through a series of difficult events. Those setbacks are different for everyone. But they always happen. They are part of the "ideal career" process on your way to becoming a Happy High Achiever: from defining what freakin' amazing looks like for you, to figuring out how to create and work with reach-out emails, to negotiating and getting your ideal organization to change the job offer to suit you.

It's never just one thing (or two or three). Which is why making a change to your ideal career is so hard.

It took one year from the time Vicky contacted me until she accepted her ideal offer, which was in LA and in treasury, right where she wanted to be. She worked hard to make the transition, and as a gift to herself, she scheduled her first day of work on her birthday.

Whether you want to start on your birthday or decide to wait until Canadian Thanksgiving, there's one thing I can guarantee: just like Vicky, Stephanie, and Adam, you will have setbacks in your journey toward your ideal career. They will show up in unexpected and surprising ways. But they are worth working through because on the other side of those setbacks is a different life. Beyond the grueling marathons and the high brick walls lies the land of the thriving, an exclusive club where people enjoy their work enough to begin a new role even on their birthday.

But what does thriving look like? And more importantly, once you find the right opportunity, how do you keep thriving? In the next chapter, we'll cover what stops people from thriving even when they have a unicorn opportunity that matches up with their Ideal Career Profile. Yes, it can still happen.

Happen To Checklist

Answer these questions:

☐ How long do you expect your career change to take?

☐ Will you be okay if setbacks affect this expectation?

☐ Many people anticipate their experiments will go perfectly. What will you do when they don't?

Happen To Bonus

Find the link to Vicky's full story (and all the other stories) at the end of this book.

18

Learning to Thrive in Your Career

My mission in life is not merely to survive,
but to thrive; and to do so with some passion, some
compassion, some humor, and some style.

MAYA ANGELOU

M Y FAMILY and I love to travel. In 2016 we started traveling internationally for four to six weeks at a time. It was a way for us to explore many of the places Alyssa and I had wanted to visit for years, and also to educate our kids about appreciating different cultures, experiences, and human differences.

Sometimes this was a trip where we traveled but also worked and the kids did their schoolwork online (just doing life in another country). Other times this was a complete vacation. I've learned over the years that when I tell people that we do this as a family every year, it sounds idyllic. In many ways it is, and I'm very thankful to have created a life and career that allows me to do this.

Also, I've found that even if you have the ideal situation, it doesn't mean you can enjoy it. For example, when we went to the UK for a month, we arrived in London, jetlagged and exhausted. For the next two weeks we struggled unsuccessfully to adapt to the different time zone and new situation. Alyssa wasn't sleeping and eventually became ill. I was stressed because I was too tired to get work done.

We had spent all this time and effort to be able to travel and we weren't even enjoying it. We couldn't shake the old time zone, couldn't adapt to the new environment, and were snapping at the kids who were also trying to adapt. So, we changed our plans and went to a beach house on the coast of Ireland so that we could relax and avoid needing a vacation from our month-long vacation.

Now I recognize that many people might think, How bad could it be? After all, you were in the UK for a month and mostly away from work. Yes, this is true, and I fully recognize how privileged we are to be able to do this. At the same time, I learned that you can absolutely do all the work to create a great situation but not be able to enjoy it unless you can adapt. In our case, the simple fact that we were unable to adapt to the new time zone left us not enjoying life much for the first couple weeks of the trip.

The same thing can happen for your career change. You can get to a new situation that's right for you, but if you're still bringing old behaviors and old ways of operating at work to your new situation, it can be counterproductive—or even detrimental.

When people begin the process of a career change (and even before they begin), their worst fear is often, What if I do all this work but it's still not a fit? What if I'm just in the same position that I was in before, and only the names and the company have changed? If you follow the process I've laid out for you in this book, you're unlikely to have that happen. You'll be able to get there.

But there's potentially a far bigger issue at stake here. What if you get it right but you're unable to thrive in the new environment? What if you get everything you wish for, but your old behaviors and expectations make work bad for you and the people you work with? What if it's you and not them?

The good news (and the terrible news) is that it's *always* you. Even when you find the right opportunity for you, one that fits your idea of the unicorn opportunity, there will always be a high degree of chance that you won't thrive in the new career change. Unless, of course, you're prepared going in. It isn't enough to simply find the opportunity. You must change your behaviors to allow yourself to thrive in the new, better situation.

Here are some of the most common areas where old behaviors can kill a unicorn, and some suggestions on how to do it differently.

Drawing Boundaries Around Work

We tend to want to please and impress the new people in our lives. When you agree to come into a "one-time meeting" at 6:30 pm during the first week, you're already signaling to your boss and coworkers how to work with you and what your boundaries are.

Perhaps you default to old behavior and say something like, "Yes, absolutely I can come in for that meeting. Normally 6:30 pm is hard for me, but as long as it's not the norm, let's do it." Instead, try this: "I would love to have that meeting. I have family obligations at 6:30 pm every day. Let's find a different time that works for both of us."

That's thriving!

Asking for What You Want ... in the Right Way

One of the biggest reasons people never get what they want is simply that they never ask. For example, did you know that you could ask to increase your salary and time off, and even redefine your role, just six months into the position?

Instead of accepting whatever you get or don't get at the time reviews are done, try asking this: "How could we increase my salary over the next six months?" This is far better than not asking. But just barely. It takes you from exactly a zero percent chance to a marginally increased chance, but it's still not exhibiting skills and behaviors that allow you to thrive. This is because it's not specific enough and it's not asked in a way that will allow someone to say yes to it.

Here's how that might sound differently if you up your skills and adapt yourself to thrive in the new environment: "My personal goal is to be earning $23,000 more in base salary six months from now. I want to be getting such great results that it becomes a no-brainer for you and your boss to pay me that much more. Could we sit down during the first month to define specifically what it would take to make it a no-brainer? I will do all the coordination, prep, and work. I'm not asking for you to commit to paying me more right now, but instead working with me to figure out what it would take. Would you be open to this?"

You can see that this is far more specific. In this case you have defined what you're asking for and even what you are not asking for. You didn't even ask for the $23,000 to be paid out. Instead, you made what you wanted clear and then asked for only the first step to make that possible. The ask was something that your new boss could say yes to.

Learning the right way to ask is a huge skill set in itself, as is learning that the context of every situation is different. Working with a career coach who's highly skilled in communication, psychology, and negotiation is a great way to figure out the right way to ask for your situation. In this case, this kind of request can work well if you're asking after you've negotiated part of your job offer but before you've accepted the offer, so you can ask for a higher amount of compensation than what they countered with.

Your Ideal Career Is Evolving

After you've done all the great work to identify your ideal career and make it happen, you will find that drawing boundaries and investing in building other skill sets and behaviors will enhance your quality of life. I want you to legitimately enjoy your work. It's absolutely life-changing when you're getting just as much back from your career as you're giving to it. But I also want you to know that even when you get to your ideal career, this isn't the end.

Remember Laura Morrison? She was the disenchanted manager who talked to a ton of people during her social Goldilocks experiment. Four years later, I exchanged emails with her, and she said that she "was thinking about her next career move." Did that mean that her ideal career opportunity hadn't worked out? Did it mean she regretted her career change or that four years later it was all for nothing? Of course not!

Happy High Achievers know that there will always be change, iteration, and evolution. Laura was no longer growing in the way she had wanted to be when she'd made her first career change to product management. Even though she had four years of great growth and a wonderful experience at The Predictive Index, her need for growth had evolved. This is a good thing.

Your season of life will change, and what you want will change. What was once exciting to you will become less so, and you might crave variety. Or something will happen that you can't predict. Tanya Malcolm-Revell got her dream job with her number-one company, Wanderlust. After less than a year, company circumstances beyond her control turned a wonderful situation into a terrible one. Eric made a career change and then did so again a few years later when he left project engineering for teaching.

No situation stays the same forever. If it did, it would eventually become less great. Does this mean you should plan on making a career change every eighteen months, like I did in my twenties? Nope. It does mean that once you get to your new opportunity, the journey isn't over. Your new way of life is just beginning.

Happy High Achievers know that you don't have to make massive changes every year. Tiny steps toward career change work just as well if you're continually experimenting, tweaking, and refining on an ongoing basis. I pull out my Ideal Career Profile and update it once a quarter at a minimum. I'll make comments on it so I can see how it's changed over time, and I give our clients open access to my profile so that they can see how progression happens in real life.

What creates fulfilling work for every person evolves. It's not a destination, as so many people believe. It's more like your favorite app on your phone that continually fixes bugs that aren't working quite right, releasing small updates and versions to make it better and better each passing month.

In Laura's case, she said she now feels well prepared to take her next step because of her previous career-change experience. When events at Tanya's company turned her unicorn into a donkey, she was able to take what she had learned through her career-change experience, add her revised knowledge of what she wanted from her work experience, and use it to find something even better than she had imagined just a year before. That's the way making a career change can work for you.

I want you to continually unpack more happiness and meaning in your work and all areas of your life. But this isn't just for you. In the introduction I told you about my secret mission in writing this book. It's bigger than you. We all need you to figure out what makes your work more fulfilling. Then we all need you to align yourself with an opportunity or organization that fits. If that doesn't work, create your own. (Yet another book!) We need you to be successful so that you can show others how it can be possible to work in ways that fit them and are healthier, happier, and so much more purposeful. Although the stats around how many people love their job are dismal at the time I'm writing this book, my hope is that in ten years I will need to edit that statement out in a new version of this book because it's no longer relevant.

I would love your help to change the way we as humans do work so that it's much easier to thrive in our careers. The most important thing you can do is to get yourself there. Use this book to determine the milestones for your plan. Create your plan for inevitable success. Get the help you need. Determine your personal ideals, experiment, and learn to thrive and adapt in your new environment. Do this for yourself. Do this for the people you care about. Do this to role model for future generations that work can be less like, well, work, and much more like a tool that provides meaning, purpose, and contribution for you and everyone around you.

Your "Why"

There's no Happen To Checklist at the end of this chapter. Instead, I want you to do something else: email me directly at scott@happentoyourcareer.com and put "My why" in the subject line.

I want you to tell me why it's important for you to commit to making your career change to meaningful work. My team and I read every single email and get back to as many people as we possibly can.

I can't wait to hear about the impact you have on the world with your commitment!

How to get started now (not later) with your career change

CAN'T GET enough and want to design your own ideal career? Here are the very best places to get started:

Podcast
The *Happen to Your Career Podcast*: Subscribe on any podcast player by searching "Happen to Your Career" and clicking subscribe or visit happentoyourcareer.com/podcast

Bonuses
All of the resources mentioned in this book are available for free at happentoyourcareer.com/bonus

Connect with Scott
Don't forget to send your "why" to scott@happentoyourcareer.com (why is it important to you to commit to making the change to meaningful work?). Add "my why" in the subject line.

If you loved this book, please consider leaving a review on your favorite online retailer—it helps so many other people decide to read it and make their own career change. ★ ★ ★ ★ ★

Acknowledgments

EVERY AUTHOR seems to say, "This book would not have been possible without . . ." followed by a long list of people. I now understand fully why. It's borderline ridiculous that only my name is on the front cover, because the work of so many people went into producing this book and bringing it to life. It's only by necessity that we stuck with my name, because there literally would not be enough room to represent all the people behind the real production of this book.

You know who you are, but just in case you don't, thank you to:

Dave Stachowiak for saying yes to being my accountability buddy years ago and for keeping me on track with the book both daily and even right meow!

Pete Mockaitis for pushing my interest to use spreadsheets, data, and technology to the extreme—it influenced everything from the words we chose to use to the color of the cover.

Kwame Christian for continuing to challenge me to see what's possible and inspiring me to go really big.

Chris Deferio for always getting me to think about the things I never, ever would have thought of.

Lisa Lewis Miller for helping me develop and test many of these ideas in the early days (and coming up with the name for the Social Goldilocks experiment!).

Dan, Michael, Haley, Kristy, Eric, Linnea, Maggie, Stephanie, Tanya, James, Cheri, Vicky, Adam, Larry, Jenny, Mike, Bowe, Samit, Jessica, and Laura for working so hard on your own career change and allowing me to share your stories in the book to help so many others do what you've done.

The group of early readers who helped shape this book and provided feedback the entire way, especially Daniel Johnson, Brian Van, Limari Navarrete, Lea Schlosser, Nancy Manley, Mia Chen, Daniel, Shannon Ripple, Nina Hess, Scott Ingham, Sara Schumann, Eric Rosen, Johannah Ridley Casseus, Karl Schwartz, Michelle Forgette, David Leib, Bill Hanafin, Christine Kapperman, Maureen White, Quynh Kilpack, Nancee-Laetitia, Lynn Delaney, Safiya Robinson, Marisa McGill, Greta Castelli, and Rachael Flug.

Josh Rivers for choosing to be there in the beginning, seeing something in HTYC, and helping us go from nothing to something. Also, for being involved in every aspect of it. I'm forever grateful!

Mark Sieverkropp for being my partner in crime when HTYC was just a project and a blog and helping to create the eight-day mini-course and for countless stories that make me laugh. Thanks for being the kind of friend where we can always just pick up where we left off.

Phillip Migyanko for coming to that live podcast recording in SXSW Austin and staying after they shut down the alcohol and everyone else left! More importantly, for showing me the value of relating to other humans and fiercely defending the HTYC ideals (even when I'm unintentionally working against them). Also, for calling out that this book is about doing, finding, and creating work unconventionally. (It's now even in the subtitle. Yay!)

Kate Wilkes for organizing literally my entire life. Without your support there's no way I could have created the time to make this book happen. Also for being a real-life role model of culture creation and living permanently outside your comfort zone. You're truly inspiring.

Cindy, Samantha, Liz, Ang, Mo, Jennifer, and Alistair for all you've done to make this book go.

Celena Singh for stepping in to take this book to the finish line. Your caring and kindness are unparalleled, but your project management skills are a close second! ;)

Everyone at Page Two publishing—Jesse, Peter, Adrineh, Chris, and Caela—for all your help! Also Jenny for correcting all of my grammar and punctuation. It was invaluable and badly needed. Your reward is an out-of-place comma I'm adding right here that you can't correct ,

Sarah Brohman, the fairy dust that you sprinkled (or dumped by the bucket) over the manuscript changed everything. Without your coaching, editing, and daring changes, this book would not have turned out to be something I am proud of.

Alyssa, without you there would be nothing. No book, no HTYC, nothing. Without you, I would probably just be living in my mom's basement eating ketchup-flavored potato chips. You are my everything. Your dedication to making this possible amazes me. I can't count the number of times when you took the kids to sports, school, or something else so that we could create just a little extra writing or editing time. This wouldn't have ever happened without you, and any dent or change this book makes in the world and how humans work should really be attributed to you. Thank you for making this possible!

Mackenzie, Camden, and Grayson, thank you for being my reason for writing this. I want the world you grow up in to normalize work in a way that allows you to truly experiment and thrive in your career. Stay curious forever!

To our clients at HTYC, it's your stories and challenges that inspire me. You're the reason this exists. Our team mentions weekly that we must have the best clients in the world.

Lastly, thanks to you for reading this. If you've made it this far, please consider leaving a rating and review on Amazon or wherever you purchased this book. It helps so many other people find and decide to read the book.

Notes

1. Why You Must Change

1 *2018 Global Great Jobs Briefing*, Gallup, 2018, news.gallup.com/reports/ 233375/gallup-global-great-jobs-report-2018.aspx.

3. The Five Hidden Obstacles to Change

1 A. Peter McGraw, Jeff T. Larsen, Daniel Kahneman, and David Schkade, "Comparing Gains and Losses," *Psychological Science* 21, no. 10 (2010): 1438–45, doi.org/10.1177/0956797610381504; Eldad Yechiam, "The Psychology of Gains and Losses: More Complicated than Previously Thought," *Psychological Science Agenda*, APA Science Directorate, January 2015, apa.org/science/about/psa/2015/01/gains-losses.

2 "Jeff Bezos at the Economic Club of Washington (9/13/18)," CNBC, September 13, 2018, YouTube video, 1:09:57, youtube.com/ watch?v=xv_vkAOjsyo.

4. Begin with the End

1 For more on this observation, read Thomas J. Stanley and William D. Danko, *The Millionaire Next Door* (New York: Pocket Books, 1996).

2 Gallup Organization, *The Gallup Poll: Public Opinion 2012* (Lanham, MD: Rowman & Littlefield, 2014), 474.

5. Plan for Inevitable Success

1 Emilie Wapnick, "Why Some of Us Don't Have One True Calling," April 2015, TEDxBend video, 12:17, ted.com/talks/ emilie_wapnick_why_some_of_us_don_t_have_one_true_calling.

2 Eric S. Kim et al., "Association between Purpose in Life and Objective Measures of Physical Function in Older Adults," *JAMA Psychiatry* 74, no. 10 (2017): 1039–45, doi.org/10.1001/jamapsychiatry.2017.2145.

3   Angela Duckworth, *Grit: The Power of Passion and Perseverance* (New York: Scribner, 2016), 146.

4   Amy Morin, "Why Vision Boards Don't Work (and What You Should Do Instead)," *Inc.*, November 16, 2018, inc.com/amy-morin/science -says-your-vision-board-actually-decreases-chances-of-living-your -dreams-heres-what-to-do-instead.html.

9. Flexibility and Autonomy

1   Christian Albus, "Psychological and Social Factors in Coronary Heart Disease," *Annals of Medicine* 42, no. 7 (2010): 487–94, doi.org/ 10.3109/07853890.2010.515605; Andrew Courtwright, "Health Disparities and Autonomy," *Bioethics* 22, no. 8 (2008): 431–39, doi.org/10.1111/j.1467-8519.2008.00671.x.

2   Johannes Siegrist, Karin Siegrist, and Ingbert Weber, "Sociological Concepts in the Etiology of Chronic Disease: The Case of Ischemic Heart Disease," *Social Science and Medicine* 22, no. 2 (1986): 24–53, doi.org/ 10.1016/0277-9536(86)90073-0; S.G. Haynes and M. Feinleib, "Women, Work, and Coronary Heart Disease: Prospective Findings from the Framingham Heart Study," *American Journal of Public Health* 70, no. 2 (1980): 133–41, doi.org/10.2105/AJPH.70.2.133; Brie Weiler Reynolds, "FlexJobs 2018 Annual Survey: Workers Believe a Flexible or Remote Job Can Help Save Money, Reduce Stress, and More," FlexJobs, n.d., flexjobs.com/blog/post/flexjobs-2018-annual-survey-workers -believe-flexible-remote-job-can-help-save-money-reduce-stress-more.

3   Maggie Wooll, "Autonomy at Work Is Important (Now More Than Ever)," BetterUp, December 3, 2021, betterup.com/blog/autonomy-in -the-workplace.

12. Signature Strengths

1   "Signature Strengths," VIA Institute on Character, viacharacter.org/ research/findings/signature-strengths.

2   "Who We Are," Gallup, gallup.com/corporate/212381/who-we-are.aspx.

13. Supportive People

1   Dan Ariely, *Predictably Irrational: The Hidden Forces That Shape Our Decisions* (New York: HarperCollins, 2009), 321.

2   Scott Stossel, "You and Your Friend's Friend's Friends," *New York Times*, October 1, 2009, nytimes.com/2009/10/04/books/review/Stossel-t.html.

3   Alexandra Owens, "What Is Imposter Syndrome?" PsyCom, December 22, 2021, psycom.net/imposter-syndrome.

Resources and Bonuses

N THE following list you'll find all the resources, podcasts, and books I mentioned in the text. However, if you only have time to take advantage of one resource, I encourage you to subscribe to the *Happen to Your Career Podcast*. We are consistently told by our community of Happeners that is the best free resource we offer.

Just visit happentoyourcareer.com/podcast and click on your podcast player of choice so you can subscribe to the show. Listen to a new episode every Monday. This one thing will do more to change your world and career than nearly anything else. It will solve your own personal exposure problem (the restaurant with no menu) and show you how extraordinary can become possible for you.

Also, if you'd like to get this entire list with live links, plus all the rest of the book bonuses, sent right to your email, just visit happentoyourcareer.com/bonus.

1. Why You Must Change

Michael—HTYC Podcast Episode 395: How a finance executive at a major film studio went from burnout to learning that work could actually be fun. happentoyourcareer.com/395

2. Happy High Achiever Milestones

Stephanie Bilbrey—HTYC Podcast Episode 428: With an aversion to risk and being comfortably unhappy in her role standing in her way, Stephanie found what fit her only after shifting her focus to what made work ideal for her, and moved from higher education to communication strategist. happentoyourcareer.com/428

3. The Five Hidden Obstacles to Change

Jenny—HTYC Podcast Episode 405: From research scientist to university director, it took Jenny three years to work through fears and anxieties, but she did it and landed her ideal role. happentoyourcareer.com/405

4. Begin with the End

Larry—HTYC Podcast Episode 445: Larry realized he knew all about beer and went from brewing craft beer to consulting and coaching breweries on how to be financially successful. happentoyourcareer.com/445

Kristy Wenz—HTYC Podcast Episode 406: After twenty years in PR, Kristy didn't think she could get a job in another industry. Now she travels the world, tasting wine for a living. happentoyourcareer.com/406

Cheri Thom—HTYC Podcast Episode 434: After Cheri found herself in a role she didn't love, she figured out how to overcome her fear of being unqualified and landed an ideal role. happentoyourcareer.com/434

5. Plan for Inevitable Success

Book Recommendation:

Grit: The Power of Passion and Perseverance, Angela Duckworth

Linnea—HTYC Podcast Episode 402: Linnea got four promotions in six months *while looking* for her ideal career. She did it by being unafraid to try things on for size and to ask the tough questions when she was in the interview hot seat. happentoyourcareer.com/402

6. Declare Your Priorities

Kristy Wenz—HTYC Podcast Episode 255: At the beginning of her journey, Kristy defined four major desires in her dream career: travel, wine, history, and culture. Today, she gets to work in each of those areas, but her role didn't just fall into her lap. happentoyourcareer.com/255

7. Sometimes We Only *Think* We Know What We Want

Book Recommendations:

Stumbling on Happiness, Daniel Gilbert
The Happiness Project, Gretchen Rubin
The Four Tendencies, Gretchen Rubin
Decisive, Chip Heath and Dan Heath

Eric—HTYC Podcast Episode 128: Eric was working ten-to-fourteen-hour days in his engineering role. Every single day he felt the urge to work with an organization that was giving back to the world. He had no idea that he was so far off. happentoyourcareer.com/128

8. Contribution

Cindy—HTYC Podcast Episode 451: Cindy is passionate about helping people in the first step toward finding work they love. She's also one of the first people you talk to at HTYC. happentoyourcareer.com/451

11. Growth

James Sannan—HTYC Podcast Episode 449: James faced his conflict of stagnant growth and tried to correct it by changing roles within his company. He discusses how he was able to find the growth he needed to thrive in his career. happentoyour career.com/449

12. Signature Strengths

Maggie: How to leverage your existing skills and land your dream job! happentoyourcareer.com/career-change-bootcamp-maggie

The CliftonStrengths Assessment (formerly known as Strengths-Finder 2.0 Assessment) helps you learn verbiage to articulate your strengths. Note: This assessment will not give you occupations to pursue. happentoyourcareer.com/clifton-strengths -assessment

13. Supportive People

Book Recommendation:
Predictably Irrational: The Hidden Forces That Shape Our Decisions, Dan Ariely

Dan—HTYC Podcast Episode 444: Re-evaluating his priorities, Dan learned that an executive level role wasn't right for him. Even though his new role is technically a step down, he now makes more and is able to focus on what he does best. happen toyourcareer.com/444

14. Values

Eric—HTYC Podcast Episode 450: It took Eric a whole year to find the right role. Along the way, he had to learn to ask the hard questions and say no to many "good" opportunities. happento yourcareer.com/450

16. Designing Career Experiments

Laura Morrison—HTYC Podcast Episode 421: Laura was "happily exhausted" in her career, while struggling with a newborn. This led to a shift in her priorities. She talks about how this shift occurred from deeper self-awareness and another career change. happentoyourcareer.com/421

Mike—HTYC Podcast Episode 174: Over the life of Mike's career, he has worked in many different cities. Learn what the differences are between local versus remote job searching and how career coaching can take you from being a good job candidate to a great one. happentoyourcareer.com/174

Celena—HTYC Podcast Episode 453: Celena worked in the corporate world for many years. Here's how she decided to make a career switch to early retirement. happentoyourcareer.com/453

17. Adjusting to Setbacks

Adam Bloom—HTYC Podcast Episode 437: A lawyer for many years, Adam went from career jail to learning how to set himself up to pivot into what he really wanted to be doing. happentoyourcareer.com/437

Vicky Meng—HTYC Podcast Episode 392: A finance professional with scattered experiences at the same company, Vicky was able to overcome her fears and doubts to land her ideal career in one year. happentoyourcareer.com/392

18. Learning to Thrive in Your Career

Tanya Malcolm-Revell—HTYC Podcast Episode 183: A TV producer in New York City for years, Tanya went from career burnout to landing her new career by leveraging her previous work and life experience. happentoyourcareer.com/183

Printed in Great Britain
by Amazon